MAKING KITCHEN CABINET ACCESSORIES

Custom Designs for Space Savers & Organizers

Sam Allen

 Sterling Publishing Co., Inc.   New York

Dedication

This book is dedicated to Robin and Patty Peavey.

Edited by Keith L. Schiffman

Library of Congress Cataloging-in-Publication Data

Allen, Sam.
    Making kitchen cabinet accessories: custom designs
for space savers and organizers / by Sam Allen.
       p.   cm.
    Includes index.
    1. Kitchen cabinets. I. Title.
  TT197.A452 1990
  684.1′6—dc20   90-9981
                                  CIP

10 9 8 7 6 5 4 3 2 1

© 1990 by Sam Allen
Published by Sterling Publishing Company, Inc.
387 Park Avenue South, New York, N.Y. 10016
Distributed in Canada by Sterling Publishing
% Canadian Manda Group, P.O. Box 920, Station U
Toronto, Ontario, Canada M8Z 5P9
Distributed in Great Britain and Europe by Cassell PLC
Villiers House, 41/47 Strand, London WC2N 5JE, England
Distributed in Australia by Capricorn Ltd.
P.O. Box 665, Lane Cove, NSW 2066
Manufactured in the United States of America
All rights reserved

Sterling ISBN 0-8069-5786-7 Paper

CONTENTS

Acknowledgments

I would like to gratefully acknowledge the help of my wife, Virginia Allen, in the preparation of this book. I would also like to thank Betty Allen for allowing me to use her kitchen for testing and photographing the projects in this book. Thanks are also due to the staff and directors of the Dan O'Laurie Museum of Moab, Utah for graciously allowing me to examine and photograph the Hoosier cabinet in their collection.

INTRODUCTION

Kitchen cabinet accessories can be added to standard cabinets to make them more efficient. They can range from a simple breadboard to a large island that contains many other accessories. Space in a kitchen is always at a premium. Most of this book deals with making maximum use of existing space. Chapter 1 covers work space. If counter space in your kitchen is limited, you can use the ideas in chapter 1 to add pullout work surfaces or to build an island work center. Storage space can be increased either by using existing space more efficiently, or by making use of space that is normally unused. Chapter 2 covers storage space, and among other things, you will find out how to add a cabinet in the stud cavity of a wall, or how to make better use of an existing cabinet by adding a shallow cabinet to the door.

The modern kitchen is full of appliances. Finding a convenient place to store them can become a problem. Chapter 3 covers appliance space. You will find ideas for appliance storage areas that will both keep appliances handy for use and that will eliminate clutter on the counter.

An efficient kitchen can also please the eye. Chapter 4 covers display space; here you will learn how to add spaces that can be used to display your fine china or decorative items.

An organized kitchen can be much easier to use than one

Illus. 1. The Hoosier cabinet, a kitchen accessory of the late 1800s, incorporated many ingenious design innovations. Modern cabinet designers have adapted some of these features for use in built-in cabinetry.

where you have to rummage through cluttered shelves and drawers. Chapter 5 covers organizers; here you will find various accessories that will help you keep your kitchen organized.

Many of the projects in this book are based on ideas incorporated in one of the first mass-produced kitchen accessories, the Hoosier cabinet (Illus. 1). Kitchens of the late 1800s and early 1900s lacked most of the modern conveniences we take for granted today. Many didn't have any built-in cabinetry. The freestanding Hoosier cabinet was designed to combine as many functions as possible into a single unit. This led to some ingenious innovations. The countertop pulled out to add work space when needed. Roll-up tambour doors hid clutter when closed, but opened out of the way when the space was needed. Spice racks and hangers on the insides of doors added

Illus. 2. These four simple joints are used in most of the projects described in this book.

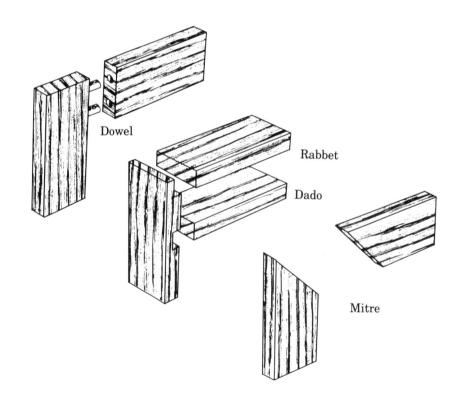

Dowel

Rabbet

Dado

Mitre

Illus. 3. A dowelling jig guides the drill bit to make a straight and accurately placed dowel hole.

Illus. 4. Dowel centers can be used to mark the location of dowel holes on the mating part.

useful storage space and kept things organized.

As built-in cabinets became more common, many of the innovations in the Hoosier cabinet were forgotten. Today, with smaller kitchens and more appliances, the need for efficient use of space has led kitchen designers to adapt many of the ideas found in the Hoosier to modern built-in cabinets.

Projects

The projects in this book are designed to be built using hand tools or some basic power equipment, such as a table saw, router or sabre saw. You need some basic woodworking skills to build the projects, but you don't need to be a master cabinetmaker. Even if you don't feel confident building one of the projects yourself, this book will give you some ideas that you can incorporate into your plans when you have someone else remodel your kitchen. The best time to add accessories is when you are installing new cabinets, but most of the projects in this book have been designed so that you can add them to existing cabinets.

The dimensions given in the project plans will fit many existing cabinets, but be sure to measure the space available and to modify the dimensions if necessary.

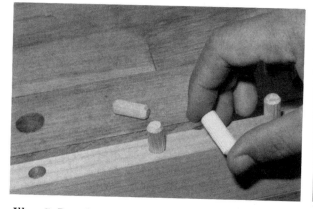

Illus. 5. Dowel pins with straight flutes help to spread the glue evenly throughout the joint. The chamfered ends make insertion easier.

Illus. 6. A stack dado blade consists of two separate blades and a variety of chippers that fit between the blades. The width of cut is determined by the size and number of chippers used.

To keep construction simple, most of the projects are designed using four simple joints: the *dowel joint, rabbet, dado,* and *mitre.* (Illus. 2). The dowel joint is just a butt joint reinforced with dowels. All of the projects in this book that use dowel joints use blind dowel joints. In a blind joint, the dowel is completely hidden when the joint is assembled. Use a stop on the drill or put a piece of masking tape on the drill shank to indicate when to stop drilling so that the holes don't go all the way through the board. Aligning the holes accurately in the mating parts is important when making blind dowel joints. A dowelling jig will help get the alignment right. There are several types available; the one shown (Illus. 3) is the type I use. It has slots that can be used to guide the hole position in the mating board. You drill the first set of holes using the jig to keep the bit straight, then you clamp the first board to the mating board and insert a dowel. The slot in the jig fits over the dowel. The jig aligns the hole with the dowel so that they will match up during assembly.

Using dowel centers is another way to align the holes. These are metal plugs that fit into a dowel hole (Illus. 4). There is a small point in the center of the plug. To mark the holes, drill the holes in the first board, then insert the dowel centers. Hold the first board in position on the mating board and tap the end of the dowel center with a mallet. The points of the dowel centers will leave an impression on the mating board. Drill the holes using the marks as a center point. I use commercially made dowel pins that have straight flutes and chamfered ends (Illus. 5). The flutes help to distribute the glue evenly, resulting in a stronger joint.

To assemble a dowel joint, apply glue to the mating surfaces of the joint and drip some glue into each hole. For maximum strength, use a sliver of wood to spread the glue around inside the hole. It is most important to get a strong bond on the dowel in joints where only two dowels are used, because if one of the dowels lets go, the joint will fail. When a joint has many dowels, you usually can't spread the glue in each hole before the glue begins to set; in that case, just drip the glue into the hole and let the flutes on the dowel distribute the glue. Don't use too much glue in the holes or you might not be able to get the dowel to go in all the way. Forcing the dowel into the joint can create pressure that may split the board, so apply just enough glue to coat the interior of the hole.

Rabbets and dadoes can be made on a table saw using a dado blade. The dado blade can be adjusted to make a cut wider than a normal blade. There are two types of dado blades. The *stack dado* uses two blades and various chippers (Illus. 6). The chippers fit between the blades, and the size of the cut is determined by which chippers you use. Small ad-

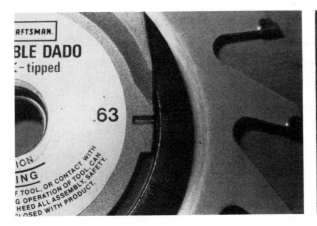

Illus. 7. A wobbler dado blade is adjusted by aligning a scale division with an index mark. The width of cut can be easily adjusted to any dimension within the range of the blade.

Illus. 8. When making a rabbet in the end of a narrow board, use the mitre gauge to guide the cut.

Illus. 9. To cut a rabbet along the edge of a board, use the rip fence as a guide. A piece of wood clamped to the fence is needed to keep the blade from hitting the metal fence.

Illus. 10. When cutting a dado in a narrow board, use the mitre gauge to guide the cut.

justments in size can be made by adding paper washers between the chippers. The other type of dado blade is called a *wobbler* (Illus. 7). The blade fits in an assembly that causes the blade to wobble back and forth. The more wobble there is, the wider the cut will be. The size of the cut is adjusted by rotating one part of the assembly. A scale gives you an approximate indication of the size of the cut. Either type of blade can be used to make the joints used in this book. When you use a dado blade on plywood, there is a tendency for the face veneer of the plywood to chip along the cut. You can minimize the chipping by first applying masking tape along the line of the cut before you make the cut. In severe cases of chipping, you can score a line with a sharp utility knife before making the cut. Score through the first layer of veneer. When you make the cut, make sure that the scored line is just barely on the outside of the blade.

A rabbet is used to join two boards at a corner. To make the rabbet, set the dado blade to make a cut wider than the width of the rabbet. When the rabbet is on the end of a narrow board, you can use the mitre gauge to guide the cut (Illus. 8). For rabbets in the long edge of a board, use the fence. Attach a piece of wood to the rip fence of the saw. Most fences will have holes provided to drive screws through the fence into the auxiliary wood fence. The auxiliary fence protects the blade from hitting the metal fence. Lower the blade below the table and position the wood fence so that it covers part of the blade. Now turn on the saw and raise the blade slowly. This will cut a pocket in the fence. Turn off the saw and adjust the blade height to the depth of the rabbet. Move the fence so that the exposed portion of the blade is equal to the width of the rabbet. You are now ready to cut the rabbet in the board. Place the face of the board on the table and the edge against the fence. Push the board through; keep your hands away from the line of the cut (Illus. 9).

A dado is used to join two boards when they don't meet at a corner. The dado blade is set to the width of the dado and the blade is raised to the proper height to get the desired depth of cut. When the board is narrow, guide it with the mitre gauge (Illus. 10). If the board is large, use the fence to guide the cut (Illus. 11). A groove is a similar joint that runs *with* the grain of the board. It is cut the same way.

The mitre joint hides the end grain of both boards. The joint is cut at 45°. You can use the mitre gauge on a table saw to cut the mitre. Set the gauge to 45° (Illus. 12). Adding a wood extension to the mitre gauge makes it easier to guide long boards. Sandpaper glued to the face of the mitre gauge

Illus. 11. When cutting a groove in a long board, guide the cut with the rip fence.

Illus. 12. When using a mitre joint to join two boards at a right angle, the mitre gauge is set to 45°.

Illus. 13. A wood extension attached to the mitre gauge is helpful when working with longer boards. Sandpaper attached to the board keeps the work from slipping during the cut.

Illus. 14. Mitre joints can be cut by hand. A mitre box guides the saw to make an accurate 45° cut.

extension will help keep the board from slipping during the cut (Illus. 13).

A mitre box is useful when cutting a mitre by hand. It is a guide that has slots for the saw. The slots are cut at 45° so that they can be used to guide the saw (Illus. 14). A mitre joint needs some reinforcement to give it strength. For the projects in this book, you can simply nail the joint together. Drill pilot holes with a bit that is slightly smaller than the nail size. Apply glue to the joint and assemble, then drive the

Illus. 15. Bar clamps are used when gluing cutting boards and butcher blocks. Alternate the clamps from top to bottom to avoid cupping as the clamps are tightened. Strips of scrap wood placed between the clamp and the work will prevent the jaws of the clamps from denting the work.

Illus. 16. Exposed plywood edges look better if they're covered with wood veneer tape. First apply contact cement to the plywood edges and to the back of the tape.

nails into the pilot holes. Use finish nails and set the head slightly below the surface.

Some of the projects will require assembly with clamps. Bar clamps that use standard black pipe for the bar are inexpensive and can be purchased at most home center stores. You need at least three bar clamps (Illus. 15).

Plywood is used in several projects. The projects will look better if you cover the exposed edges of the plywood with wood veneer tape. The tape is made from real wood, and you can buy it to match the face veneer of the plywood. A paper backing on the tape gives it strength and flexibility. The tape is applied with contact cement, or you can get a heat-sensitive type that is applied with a hot iron.

To apply the tape, cut a piece with scissors to the approximate length needed. Apply contact cement to the plywood edge and to the back of the tape (Illus. 16) and let the cement dry. Position one end of the tape on the plywood, leaving an overhang on the end and both edges. Press the tape down as you work toward the other end. Use a block of wood to press the tape firmly against the plywood, then trim. You can use

Illus. 17. When the contact cement is dry, press the tape in place. Use scissors to cut off large overhangs.

scissors to remove some of the overhang (Illus. 17). A sharp utility knife will remove the rest (Illus. 18). Use 150 grit sandpaper wrapped around a small block of wood to sand the tape flush with the face of the plywood, then angle the block slightly and bevel the edge of the tape (Illus. 19).

Illus. 18. A sharp utility knife can be used to trim the tape to exact size.

Illus. 19. A piece of sandpaper wrapped around a block of wood can be used to remove any remaining overhang. Hold the sanding block at an angle to bevel the edges slightly. The bevel makes it less likely that the tape will be pulled loose by getting snagged.

When two pieces of tape will join at a corner, you can make a mitre joint. Apply one piece of tape first, then apply the second one overlapping the first at the corner. Use a combination square to guide a sharp utility knife. Cut through

Illus. 20. To mitre the tape at a corner, apply both pieces with the second one overlapping the first. Use a combination square to guide a utility knife and make a 45° cut through both pieces of tape.

Illus. 21. Peel back the overlapping piece of tape and remove the waste.

Illus. 22. Press the tape back down, and you should have a perfect mitre joint.

both pieces of tape (Illus. 20). Peel back the tape and remove the waste (Illus. 21). Press the tape back down and you should have a perfect mitre joint (Illus. 22).

Safety

When you build one of the projects, don't let an accident mar your enjoyment. Be sure to observe all safety practices recommended by the tool manufacturer. Wear eye protection when there is the possibility that a foreign object may get into your eye. Use the safety guards that come with the power tools. Use a push stick to keep your fingers away from power saw blades. Tie back long hair to keep it out of rotating equipment, and avoid jewelry and loose clothing that can get tangled in machinery. Don't ever work when you are under the influence of alcohol or drugs; even prescription drugs can dull your reactions, so ask your doctor if it is safe to use power equipment while you are taking a medication. If you keep safety in mind as you work, you can have fun and work more efficiently.

1
WORK SPACE

Work space is one of the most precious commodities in a kitchen: no matter how much you have, you could always use more. This chapter contains projects that either add to the usable work space, or make better use of existing space. One way to get additional work space is to use *hideaway units*. These can be pulled out for additional counter space when needed, and stored away when not in use. A traditional bread-board is a simple example. The Hoosier cabinet solved the problem with a slide-out counter. The amount of work space could be doubled by pulling out the steel countertop (Illus. 23). A kitchen island can provide more counter space and additional storage. In some instances, a section of countertop could be put to better use if you could set hot pans on it, or if it could be used as a cutting board. In this case, a built-in insert can be installed.

Illus. 23. Work space is a precious commodity in a kitchen. The Hoosier cabinet incorporated a slide-out counter to increase the available work space.

Breadboards, Cutting Boards & Chopping Blocks

One of the basic kitchen cabinet accessories is the breadboard. It pulls out from the base cabinet to give added work space (Illus. 24). Cutting boards and chopping blocks are similar to breadboards, but they are designed for cutting meat. A breadboard can also be used to provide a temporary work surface that can be pulled out when needed, and hidden away when not in use. These accessories add a considerable amount of work area without taking up all of the available floor space. Projects used to increase available work space can vary in size and complexity from a simple pullout work surface not much different from a breadboard, to a sturdy pullout table. A place near the range to put hot pans is a necessity. A pullout covered with ceramic tile or stainless steel is a good solution.

A traditional breadboard is made of solid lumber strips glued together to the width desired. Because the wood is subject to a lot of moisture, take special precautions when

Illus. 24. A breadboard is a simple way to increase the available work space.

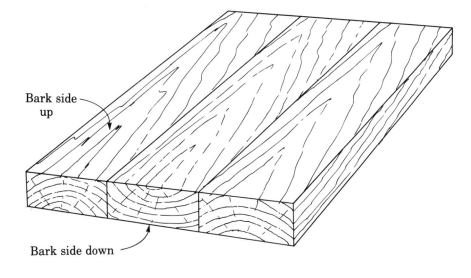

Illus 25. When gluing a breadboard, alternate the rings to minimize cupping.

Bark side up

Bark side down

making a breadboard. First glue together the stock using a water-resistant glue. In most cases, aliphatic resin (yellow carpenter's glue) can be used; for a very durable board, use epoxy. Alternate the growth rings of the boards to minimize cupping. To do this, look at the end grain of the board and

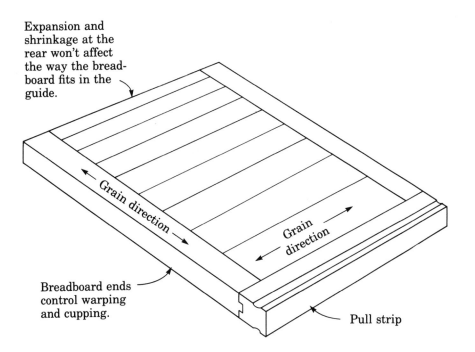

Illus. 26. Breadboard ends can help to avoid cupping. Breadboard ends are usually used at the front and back of a breadboard. When they are placed on the sides, as shown here, they also prevent jamming in the guides caused by dimensional change across the width of the board.

Expansion and shrinkage at the rear won't affect the way the breadboard fits in the guide.

Grain direction

Grain direction

Breadboard ends control warping and cupping.

Pull strip

note the curvature of the rings. Arrange the boards so that the curve faces the opposite direction in alternating boards. The side of the board that was closest to the outside of the tree is called the *bark side;* this side has the largest rings. Place the boards so that the bark side alternates from one board to the next (Illus. 25).

To further minimize cupping, a breadboard end is used. These are boards attached to both ends of the breadboard with the grain running at a right angle to the grain in the rest of the boards. A tongue and groove joint is usually used to attach the ends. Wood will swell when it gets wet and shrink as it dries; most of the change in size will occur across the width of the board. This process is called *dimensional change.* Dimensional change can be a problem in a kitchen's wet environment. If the breadboard swells, it can jam in the guide. Shrinkage can lead to cracks and loose joints. Breadboard ends can solve these problems; but if you don't apply the ends correctly, you can exaggerate the problem. Breadboard ends can be used to keep the board from jamming in the guide (Illus. 26). The boards in the center are aligned

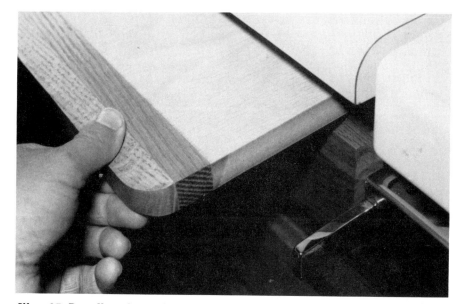

Illus. 27. Breadboards can be made of plywood or particleboard. A hardwood face veneer can be used as shown here; but for greater durability, cover the plywood or particleboard with plastic laminate.

Illus. 28. A cutting board is like a breadboard, but it is thicker, and a harder wood is used for greater durability.

Illus. 29. End-grain makes a better cutting surface because it can stand abuse better. Chopping blocks are made so that the end-grain is on the surface.

with the grain running across the width of the board, and the breadboard ends are applied to the sides. With this arrangement, the greatest amount of dimensional change will be from front to back. The change in the side-to-side dimension will be small, so there is less chance of the board jamming in the guides.

When breadboard ends are used, the board may split as it shrinks. The usual method of attaching the ends is to glue the entire length of the tongue and groove joint. If a flexible glue such as white polyvinyl acetate (PVA) is used, this is usually all right, unless there is a lot of shrinkage. When the board shrinks greatly, the glued joint resists the movement and the board may split to relieve the stress. This can be avoided by allowing some movement in the joint. To do this, use three dowels to lock the tongue and groove together while allowing some movement in the joint, or use a sliding dovetail joint. (See projects 1 and 2 at the end of this chapter.)

Plywood or particleboard can be used to make a breadboard (Illus. 27). These materials eliminate problems of cupping, shrinkage and swelling. A hardwood face veneer can also be used, but for the *best* durability, cover the board with plastic laminate. See project 3.

A cutting board is made in the same way as a breadboard, but it should be thicker and a harder wood is needed (Illus. 28). See project 4. A chopping block is made a bit differently. The wood is glued so that the end grain is on the top surface of the block. End grain can withstand abuse better than face grain (Illus. 29). You can assemble the chopping block from small individual pieces, but there is an easier method. First, edge-glue some boards together. On one edge use a narrow board so that the joints can be staggered in the finished block. Arrange the glue joints so that they don't line up. After the glue is dry, cut strips from the glued boards. The width depends upon the desired thickness of the block. The strips can then be glued together to make the block. Stagger the joints as you assemble the block by reversing every other strip. See project 5.

FINISHING

Anything used to prepare food must have a *nontoxic* finish. Breadboards, cutting boards and chopping blocks are often left unfinished. If you want the added durability of a finish, use a nontoxic penetrating oil finish. This type of finish is

Illus. 30. The simplest type of breadboard guide is made by cutting a groove in a board.

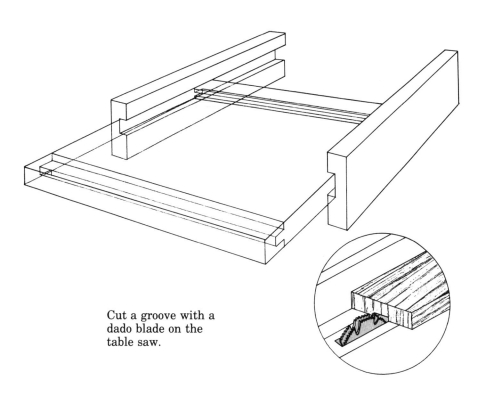

Cut a groove with a
dado blade on the
table saw.

*Illus. 31. To make the
breadboard guides, cut a
groove that is slightly
wider than the thickness
of the breadboard into
boards that will attach to
the sides of the cabinet.*

usually called *salad bowl* finish, and is available from several
manufacturers. If you can't find it locally, it can be ordered
from most mail order woodworking supply companies.

GUIDES

The simplest type of guide for a breadboard or other type of
pullout is simply a board with a groove cut in the face to
accept the edge of the breadboard (Illus. 30). This is the traditional type of guide used for most breadboards. This guide
provides adequate support provided the board isn't pulled out
too far. To make the guides, start with a board that is at least
three times wider than the thickness of the breadboard. Cut
a groove in the center of the guide using a dado blade on a
table saw. The groove should be slightly wider than the thickness of the breadboard, and the depth should be one-half the
thickness of the guide board. Attach the guides to the sides of
the cabinet so that they align with the opening for the breadboard (Illus. 31). Rub some paraffin wax on the groove to
make the breadboard slide easily. A commercial metal guide

Illus. 32. This metal guide can be used in place of the traditional wood guides.

Illus. 33. Metal drawer guides can be used when a more rigid work surface is needed. This type of guide requires more mounting area than is available on a standard breadboard, so it can only be used when the design allows for extra mounting surface.

is available that functions similarly. The advantage of the metal guide is that it is easy to install, and the breadboard can be mounted in the same opening as a drawer without the need for a rail between the breadboard and the drawer (Illus. 32).

When a more rigid work surface is needed, you can use metal drawer guides on a pullout (Illus. 33). Most guides require more mounting area than the thickness of a standard breadboard, but they work well for thicker cutting boards or chopping blocks. When you use the drawer guides with a cutting board, you can conceal the board behind a hinged drawer front. This gives the cabinet a finished look that matches the surrounding drawers (Illus. 34). The hinged drawer front can also be used to hide a standard breadboard. There will be leftover room under the board, so you can add a small drawer that is a useful storage space for knives and utensils frequently used at the breadboard (Illus. 35). Another way to get a strong work surface is to use a framework similar to a drawer. The cutting board rests on cleats attached to the side of the frame; the board can be lifted out for cleaning. Use heavy-duty metal drawer guides attached to the frame. The frame provides the required mounting surface for the guide and adds rigidity to the work surface. This system is good for making a hideaway countertop extension because it can be fully extended and can give a solid working surface that can support the weight of small appliances (Illus. 36). For a countertop extension, the top of the dummy drawer can be made from plywood or particleboard and covered with plastic laminate. If you cover the surface with ceramic tile, this type of pullout can be a useful place to set a hot pan next to the stove. See project 6.

When you want a very solid work surface (a chopping block or a place to knead dough, for example), you can add legs to a pullout (Illus. 37). The legs have casters, and they roll along the floor as the unit is pulled out. The legs are hidden behind a door when they're not in use. See project 7.

A drop leaf counter extension can be an easy way to add more counter space. The drop leaf isn't as sturdy as a pullout

Illus. 34. This cutting board is thick enough to use a metal drawer guide. A hinged drawer front conceals the cutting board when it is not in use.

Illus. 35. A hinged drawer front can also be used to conceal a standard breadboard with a small utensil drawer beneath it.

Illus. 36. You can make a strong pullout work surface by mounting a cutting board in a drawerlike framework. The cutting board rests on cleats so that it can be removed for cleaning. The sides of the frame provide enough mounting space for heavy-duty drawer guides. See project 6.

Illus. 37. For an even stronger work surface, add legs to the pullout. The legs have casters and are hidden behind the cabinet door when not in use. See project 7.

with legs, but it will support small appliances (Illus. 38). The drop leaf is supported by special hardware that is available at most home center stores. The drop leaf is only useful on the end of a cabinet, because it would cover doors or drawers if it were attached to the front, and then folded down. See project 8.

Countertop Inserts

Plastic laminate countertops have many advantages, but you can't place hot pans on them, nor can you use them as cutting boards to cut meat or vegetables, because knife marks will mar the surface. An insert of a different material can be used to add a heat-resistant surface or a cutting board in a convenient location (Illus. 39). You can buy a ready-made insert or make your own.

The secret to adding an insert is to use a sink rim. You can get sink rims in a variety of shapes and sizes at a plumbing supply store (Illus. 40). Buy the rim first, then make the insert to fit. You can make a cutting board to fit in the sink rim, or you can use a piece of plywood covered with ceramic tile or stainless steel to provide a heat-resistant surface. The insert is installed in a hole cut into the countertop. This is a good solution when you have a burned or scratched area on the countertop. Position the insert so that the damaged area will be cut out. See project 9.

Illus. 38. A drop leaf counter extension can fold down out of the way when not in use. Special hardware is needed to support the extension. See project 8.

Illus. 39. A countertop insert can be used to add a cutting board or heat-resistant surface to a plastic laminate countertop. See project 9.

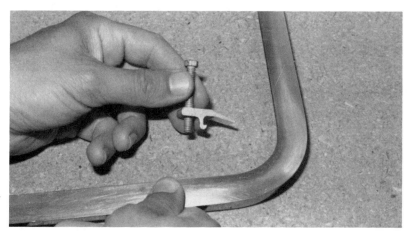

Illus. 40. A sink rim holds the insert in place. Special clips that come with the rim attach to the underside. Tightening the screw pulls the rim tight against the countertop.

Illus. 41. An island can add work space, and can provide additional storage space. When it is permanently attached, it can also be used to mount a cook top or sink.

Islands

An island is a freestanding cabinet with a countertop (Illus. 41). It can be permanently attached to the floor, with connections for plumbing and electricity, or it can be left unattached so that it can be moved. For complete mobility, casters can be added. If casters are added, they should be the locking type, so that the island can be locked in position when you are using it.

Many of the accessories described in this book can be incorporated into an island. If you are adding to an existing kitchen, this can be an excellent way to get some of the built-in accessories you want without many modifications to the existing cabinets.

There are several ways to build an island. The simplest is to use ready-made base cabinet modules and assemble them into the size you desire (Illus. 42). Since the rear of the cabinets will show, add a piece of plywood to the back and finish it to match the cabinets, or cover it with a matching plastic laminate. See project 10.

If you want to make a movable unit using modular cabinets, build the unit using overhead cabinet modules. They don't have a toe-kick, so it is easier to add casters. The casters attach to a cleat added to the bottom of the cabinets. The cleat strengthens the area where the casters attach, and it helps to hold the unit together. Using two overhead cabinets back-to-back gives you storage space on both sides of the island. A moulding will hide the joint between the two sets of cabinets. See project 11.

The island countertop can be made from any counter material. You can order a prefabricated plastic laminate countertop from a dealer, or build your own. For plastic laminate or ceramic tile, make a counter of particleboard and thicken the edges by attaching strips to the underside of the board with glue and nails. A butcher block countertop is handy, and if you don't have the tools or experience to work with plastic laminates, it will be easier to build. See project 12.

Illus. 42. Ready-made cabinet modules can be assembled into an island. See project 10.

Illus. 43. A small stowaway island can be hidden under a counter when not in use and rolled out to a convenient work location when needed. See project 13.

You can make a small movable island that stows away inside or next to stationary cabinets. If the island will fit next to an existing cabinet, make it the same height as the existing cabinet. To hide the unit under a stationary counter, the island must be shorter than the standard counter height. The front of the island can be covered with a dummy door front to make it match the rest of the cabinets when it is in the stowed position (Illus. 43). See project 13.

Projects

PROJECT 1—BREADBOARD WITH TONGUE & GROOVE ENDS

This is a basic breadboard with an end-cap to control cupping. The breadboard end is attached with a tongue and groove joint and secured with dowels in a way that permits dimensional change (Illus. 44). The choice of materials de-

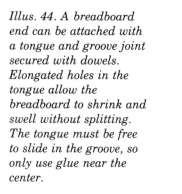

Illus. 44. A breadboard end can be attached with a tongue and groove joint secured with dowels. Elongated holes in the tongue allow the breadboard to shrink and swell without splitting. The tongue must be free to slide in the groove, so only use glue near the center.

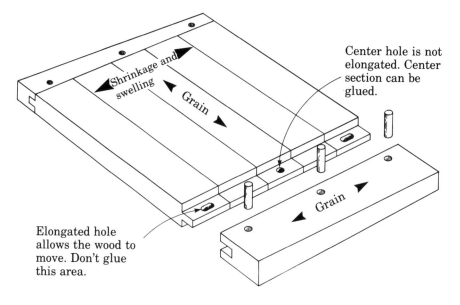

Center hole is not elongated. Center section can be glued.

Elongated hole allows the wood to move. Don't glue this area.

Shrinkage and swelling

Grain

Grain

pends on how you will use the board and how much you want to spend. Pine can be used if the board will be used mostly for rolling dough or slicing bread. For more durability, use hardwoods like alder or maple. Avoid wood (like oak) with an open grain because it is hard to clean.

Begin by cutting the boards to the rough size. Use boards that have true and square edges. Arrange the board so that the bark side alternates. Apply glue to the mating edges and clamp the panel with bar clamps. Use at least three clamps, with the two outside ones on one side and the middle one on the other. This will even out the clamping pressure and keep the board flat.

After the glue is dry, use a scraper or chisel to remove most of the excess glue, then trim the board to size allowing for the tongue on the ends. Rip the end-caps to width then put a dado blade on the table saw to cut the tongue and groove. Set the width of the cut to one-third the thickness of the board. Set the blade height to ½″. Adjust the rip fence to center the cut on the end-cap and cut the groove (Illus. 45).

To cut the tongue, add an auxiliary wood face to the fence. This prevents the blade from hitting the metal fence. Adjust

Illus. 45. Use the dado blade to cut the groove in the breadboard end-cap.

Illus. 46. Cut the tongue on the end of the breadboard using the dado blade.

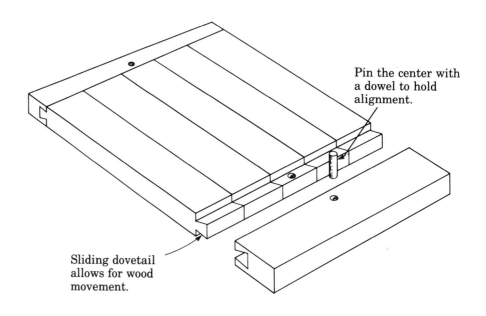

Pin the center with a dowel to hold alignment.

Illus. 47. A sliding dovetail joint gives added strength to a breadboard end joint while still allowing for dimensional change.

Sliding dovetail allows for wood movement.

the fence so that the wood face just barely clears the side of the blade. Now, put one face of the board on the table and the end against the fence and run it through the saw. Turn the board around and make a second cut on the other side. This will form the tongue (Illus. 46). Turn the board end-for-end and repeat the process.

Dry-assemble the joints and drill holes for three ⅛″ diameter dowels. Then remove the ends, and using a round file elongate the outside holes in the tongue. The center hole can be left as is. Reassemble the joints and insert dowels. The center dowel can be firmly glued in the hole; the outside dowels should be left dry for most of their length and a little glue applied to the ends to hold them in position. If the boards shrink or swell, the tongue is free to move in the groove so there won't be a problem with splitting.

Sand the board with a belt sander. If a finish is desired, use a nontoxic salad bowl finish.

PROJECT 2—BREADBOARD WITH SLIDING DOVETAIL

A breadboard end can be attached with a sliding dovetail joint. This adds strength to the joint yet it still allows for dimensional change (Illus. 47). Glue the board in the same way as described in project 1.

Rip the breadboard end to width, then set up a router to cut the joint. You will need a dovetail bit and a router table along with a router to make this joint. Adjust the depth of cut to ½″. Set the fence to center the cut. Place the end-cap against the fence and cut a dovetail groove (Illus. 48). If the router seems to have difficulty making the cut, you can cut a straight groove on the table saw first (to remove most of the waste), then run the board through the router to give the groove the dovetail shape.

After the groove is cut in both end-caps, readjust the fence to cut the dovetail on the breadboard. Move the fence until about half of the bit extends past the face of the fence. Make

Illus. 48. Cutting the dovetailed groove with a router. Use a dovetail bit in a router mounted in a router table. Guide the cut with the router table fence.

Illus. 49. The dovetail on the end of the breadboard is also cut on the router table. Readjust the fence and make a cut on both sides of the board.

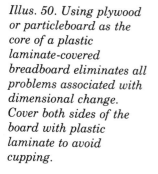

Illus. 50. Using plywood or particleboard as the core of a plastic laminate-covered breadboard eliminates all problems associated with dimensional change. Cover both sides of the board with plastic laminate to avoid cupping.

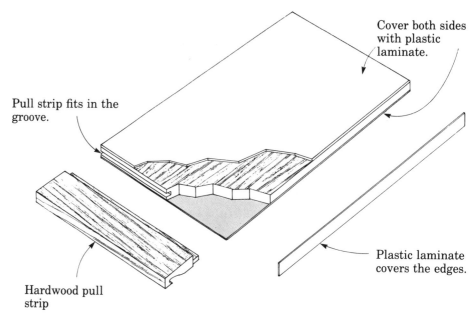

Cover both sides with plastic laminate.

Pull strip fits in the groove.

Plastic laminate covers the edges.

Hardwood pull strip

a test cut on some scrap and check the fit in the groove. When you are satisfied with the fit, make the cuts on both sides of both ends of the breadboard (Illus. 49). Assemble the joint without glue. Drill a hole in the center of the joint for a ⅛" dowel. Apply glue to the dowel and drive it into the hole. The dowel locks the joint, but the board is free to shrink and swell because it can slide in the joint on either side of the dowel.

Use a belt sander to sand the board flat and finish with salad bowl finish, if desired.

PROJECT 3—PLASTIC LAMINATE-COVERED BREADBOARD

For added durability and ease of cleaning, use plastic laminate as a surface for a breadboard. Use plywood or particleboard for the core to eliminate problems associated with dimensional change in solid wood (Illus. 50). A hardwood end-cap can be added to match the cabinets, but it isn't needed to prevent cupping. A piece of door pull moulding can be used as the end-cap to match the cabinet doors and provide a convenient finger pull (Illus. 51). Both faces of the breadboard must be covered with plastic laminate. If only one side is covered, the board may warp. It is not absolutely essential to cover the exposed plywood edges with plastic laminate, but the board will be more durable and will look better if you do.

Begin by cutting the plywood to size, then set the dado blade to cut a groove in the front edge. See project 1. In this case, the board has the groove and the pull has the tongue, because the tongue made of plywood or particleboard will break easily. Next, apply the plastic laminate to the edges of the board. Cut strips of the laminate that are about ¼″ wider than the thickness of the board. Apply contact cement to the edge of the board and to the back of the laminate. When the glue is dry, position the strip so that it overhangs equally on both sides and press it in place. Use a laminate-trimming bit in the router to trim the edges flush. It will be easier if you clamp the board to the bench so that the edge is up (Illus. 52).

Illus. 51. A piece of moulded wood cabinet pull can be attached to the end of the board.

Illus. 52. For a finished look, apply laminate to the edges of the board. Trim the overhang off using a router. A jig like the one shown here can be used to clamp the board in an upright position for trimming.

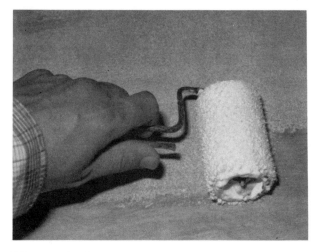

Illus. 53. Apply contact cement to both the board and to the plastic laminate. A small paint roller is a fast way to get an even coat of contact cement.

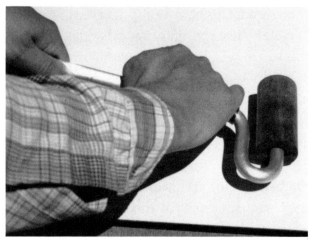

Illus. 54. After placing the laminate on the board, it must be pressed firmly in place. A "J" roller is a professional tool used for this purpose.

Next, cut the laminate for the faces. Make the piece about 1″ larger than the dimensions of the board. Apply glue to the board and to the laminate; a small paint roller makes it easy to get an even coat (Illus. 53). When the cement is dry, apply the laminate so that it overhangs all of the edges by about ½″. Apply pressure evenly over the surface to get a good bond. A "J" roller is the tool professionals use to apply pressure to the laminate. Roll over the entire surface and press down hard, but stop when you reach the overhang so you don't break it off (Illus. 54). Instead of a "J" roller, you can use a hammer and a wood block. Place the block on the surface of the laminate and hit it with the hammer. Move the block slightly and hit it again. Continue in this way until you have covered the entire surface of the board.

Clamp the board to the bench and trim the edges flush with a router and laminate-trimming bit (Illus. 55). Use a fine file to smooth the edges and bevel them slightly.

When all of the laminate has been applied, the pull strip can be glued in place. You can make a pull strip from hardwood, or you can buy a commercially milled pull like the one shown (Illus. 56). The laminate hides the ends of the groove in the breadboard. In order to have the pull strip extend all the way to the edge, you will need to trim about ⅛" from the ends of the tongue. Apply glue to the joint and clamp the pull strip to the board (Illus. 57).

PROJECT 4—CUTTING BOARD WITH DOVETAIL CLEATS

Since a cutting board is subject to more abuse than is a breadboard, it needs to be thicker, and it is usually made from a hardwood, like maple. The dovetail cleats used in this project help to resist cupping (Illus. 58).

Begin by ripping ¾" thick boards into 1½" widths. By ripping the boards to 1½", you can set them on edge as you glue the board to get a 1½" thick cutting board using ¾"

Illus. 55. Use a laminate-trimming bit in the router to trim off the overhanging laminate.

Illus. 56. The pull strip fits into a groove in the end of the board. Trim ⅛" from the ends of the tongue on the pull. This will allow the joint to be completely concealed by the laminate.

Illus. 57. Apply glue to the tongue and use bar clamps to hold the pull in place as the glue dries. Place a strip of scrap wood between the clamp jaws and the pull to avoid marring the pull.

thick lumber. It will take many strips to make the board because each strip only adds ¾″ to the width of the board. Cut the strips to length, then glue and clamp as described in project 1.

After the glue is dry, remove the clamps and scrape off the excess glue. Now, cut the sliding dovetails. First cut two ¾″ wide by ½″ deep dovetail dadoes in the underside of the board. Position them about 2″ in from the ends of the board; use a router and a dovetail bit to cut the dado. Set the router fence or clamp a board to the work to guide the cut. Make two passes to make the cut wide enough (Illus. 59).

To make the cleat, cut a strip of wood to the width of the widest part of the dovetail dado, then rip it down to ½″ thickness. Set the blade-tilt on the table saw to the angle of the dovetail bit (about 15° in most cases) and bevel the sides of the cleat (Illus. 60). Slide the cleat into the dado in the cutting board (Illus. 61). Don't use any glue. Drill a hole in the center of the cleat and partway into the cutting board for a

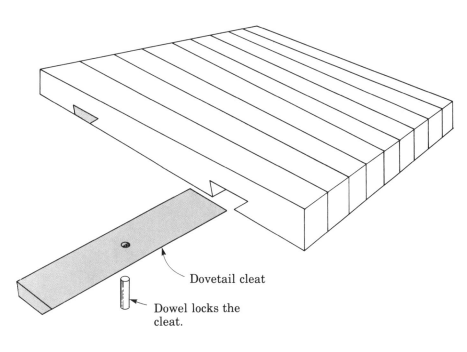

Illus. 58. A dovetail cleat on the underside of a cutting board resists cupping while allowing for expansion and contraction.

Dovetail cleat

Dowel locks the cleat.

¼″ dowel. Apply glue to the dowel and drive it into the hole. This locks the cleat in place and allows for dimensional change in the cutting board.

Use heavy-duty metal drawer guides to mount the cutting board in the cabinet. You can conceal the board behind a hinged drawer front. Attach the hinges to the lower rail of the opening (Illus. 62).

Illus. 59. Use a router and a dovetail bit to make the dovetail dadoes in the underside of the board. It will take two passes with the router to make the cut wide enough.

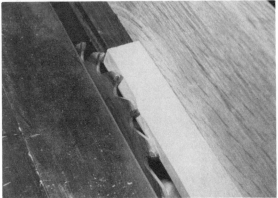

Illus. 60. Rip the cleat on the table saw with the blade tilted 15°.

Illus. 61. Slide the cleat into the dado, but don't use any glue.

PROJECT 5—CHOPPING BLOCK

A chopping block is used to chop vegetables or to cut meat. For the best durability, the wood should be arranged so that the work surface is end-grain (Illus. 63).

Begin construction by gluing together some boards in the same way as described in project 1. Use a board that is one-half the width of the other boards for the first board.

After the glue is dry, scrape off the excess glue and sand the surface smooth. Set the rip fence on the table saw to the desired thickness of the chopping block. It should be at least 1½″ thick. Put the glued board on that saw and crosscut it into strips (Illus. 64).

Apply glue to the strips and assemble the block. Arrange boards so that the joints are staggered. Remember that you used one board that was half the width of the rest when you glued the boards. By alternating the position of this narrow board, the joints will be staggered. Clamp the block and let it dry, then sand the surface with a belt sander.

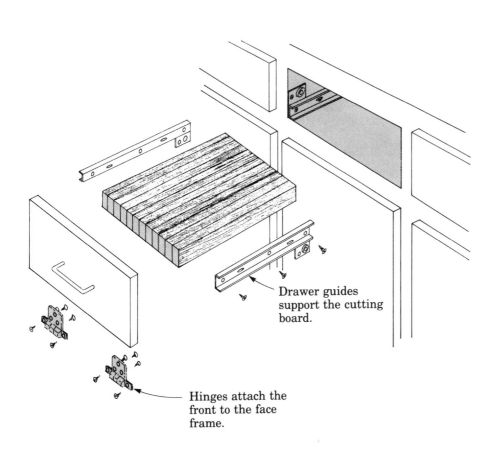

Illus. 62. Use metal drawer guides to mount the cutting board in a cabinet. Conceal the board with a drawer front hinged to the lower rail of the opening.

Drawer guides support the cutting board.

Hinges attach the front to the face frame.

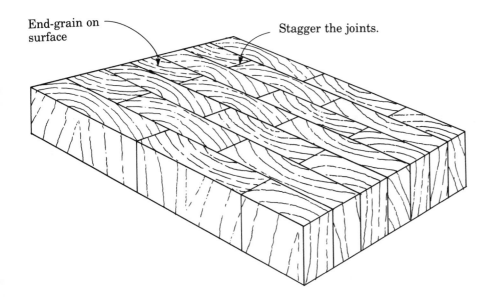

End-grain on surface

Stagger the joints.

Illus. 63. A chopping block is made with the end-grain of the boards on the surface. This arrangement is very durable when subject to knife cuts. The block is made from many small pieces glued together. Stagger the joints for strength.

Illus. 64. Instead of gluing all the individual pieces, begin by gluing a few boards edge-to-edge; then cut sections from the end of this glued panel. The sections can be glued together to form the chopping block.

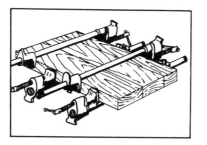

1. Glue several boards. Place a narrow board on one edge.

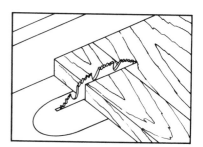

2. Crosscut the glued boards into strips.

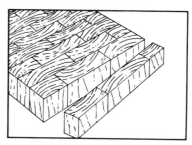

3. Apply glue to the strips and assemble. Alternate the position of the narrow board to stagger the joints.

PROJECT 6—WORK SURFACE IN A DRAWER

When you need a sturdy work surface that hides away when not in use, you can mount it in a drawer. If you already have an existing drawer that is sturdy and uses metal side guides, you can simply add a work surface. If you want to add the pullout to an area that doesn't already have a drawer, or if the existing drawer isn't sturdy enough, build a drawer frame using the accompanying plans. The work surface can be a cutting board, chopping block, ceramic tile, or plastic laminate. To add to an existing drawer, attach cleats to the inside of the drawer to support the work surface so that it's flush with the top of the drawer (Illus. 65).

The drawer frame shown (Illus. 66) is designed to support a work surface. The frame is made of ¾" thick lumber to give added strength. Most drawers are made of ½" thick or ⅜" thick lumber. There is no bottom in the drawer. This makes it easy to reach up from underneath and push out the work surface for cleaning. By eliminating the bottom, crumbs will not accumulate in the drawer.

To build the drawer frame, begin by ripping Parts A and B to width. Next cut the sides (Part A) to length. Cut a rabbet in the front end of both sides and a dado in the back. The dado is set in from the end by ¾".

Use glue and screws to attach the cleats (Part C) to the sides. Position the cleat so that the top of the work surface will be flush with the top of the side.

Apply glue to the joints and assemble the frame. Use 1½"

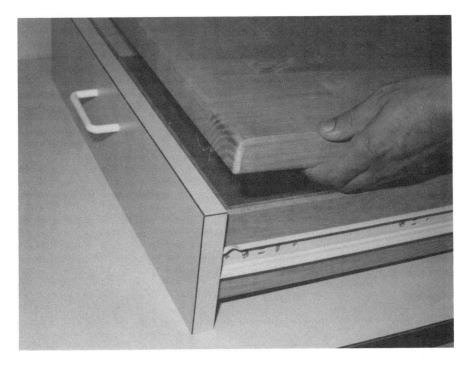

Illus. 65. Mounting a chopping block or cutting board in a drawer is an easy way to add a sturdy pullout work area.

Illus. 66. The drawer frame in this plan uses ¾" thick lumber and screws at the joints for added strength to support a work surface. You can use a cutting board (as shown), a piece of plywood covered with plastic laminate, or ceramic tile for the work surface. A strong existing drawer can be modified to support a work surface by adding cleats (Part C).

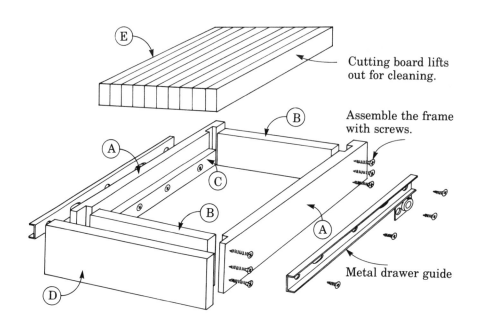

Cutting board lifts out for cleaning.

Assemble the frame with screws.

Metal drawer guide

screws to reinforce the joints. To prevent the sides from splitting, drill pilot holes before installing the screws.

Before the glue dries, set the work surface in place. If the drawer is out of square with the work surface, "rack" it until it lines up, then let the glue set.

Check the squareness of the drawer by measuring diagonally from corner to corner, then compare with the measurement across the other two corners. If the drawer is square, both measurements should be the same. If the measurements differ, you need to rack the drawer into square; do this by placing your hands on the corners that have the longest measurement and squeeze until the sides shift position a little. Remeasure the diagonals and continue to rack the drawer until the diagonals are equal.

Make a false front (Part D) for the drawer to match the rest of the drawers. Attach the front with screws driven through Part B.

Install the drawer guides following the manufacturer's directions.

Project 6
Work Surface in a Drawer

BILL OF MATERIALS

Note: Dimensions allow for ½″ clearance on sides for drawer guide.

6″ × 15″ DRAWER OPENING

Part	Description	Size	No. Req'd
A	sides	¾ × 4 × 22	2
B	front & back	¾ × 4 × 13¼	2
C	cleats	¾ × 2½ × 18¾	2
D	false front	¾ × 6 × 15	1
E	cutting board	1½ × 18⅝ × 12⅜	1

6″ × 18″ DRAWER OPENING

Part	Description	Size	No. Req'd
A	sides	¾ × 4 × 22	2
B	front & back	¾ × 4 × 16¼	2
C	cleats	¾ × 2½ × 18¾	2
D	false front	¾ × 6 × 18	1
E	cutting board	1½ × 18⅝ × 15⅜	1

PROJECT 7—HIDEAWAY TABLE

When you need a very sturdy work surface, you can add legs to the drawer frame from project 6. The result is a hideaway table. This work surface is useful as a chopping block or as a place to knead dough because you can press down hard without worrying about the strength of the surface (Illus. 67).

The plans (Illus. 68) are designed to be used with a cabinet that has no face frame and uses full overlay doors. The table legs are hidden behind a door when not in use. To extend the table, open the doors and pull out the drawer. The legs have casters; they roll along with the drawer. When the table is fully extended, the doors can be shut. Modify the existing

Illus. 67. Adding legs to the drawer frame from project 6 makes a sturdy hideaway table. When closed, the legs fit into notches cut in the shelves and are hidden by the cabinet door.

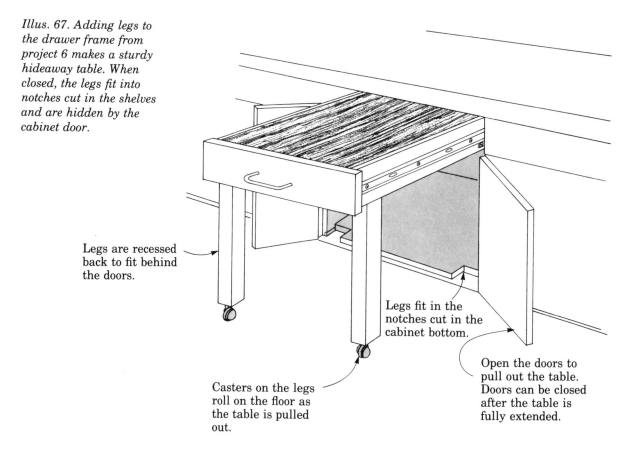

Legs are recessed back to fit behind the doors.

Legs fit in the notches cut in the cabinet bottom.

Casters on the legs roll on the floor as the table is pulled out.

Open the doors to pull out the table. Doors can be closed after the table is fully extended.

cabinet by cutting out two notches in the bottom of the cabinet back to the toe-kick so that the legs can fit inside the cabinet, behind the doors.

To build the table, follow the directions in project 6 for making the drawer frame. The only modification is that the cleat is cut back from the front to allow for the leg. Leave off the false front until after the legs are installed.

The legs are made from lumber that is 1½″ square. A fir 2 × 2 can be used, or you can use hardwood. If you can't get the wood you want in 1½″ thickness, glue two ¾″ thick pieces.

Install the casters on the legs before cutting the legs to final length. Use casters that have stems that fit into holes drilled into the bottom of the leg (Illus. 69). To find the correct length for the legs, attach the drawer guides to the frame and install the frame in the opening. Make a mark on the leg so that the top of the leg will be flush with the top of the cleat.

Finish the legs to match the cabinets. You can stain and varnish them, paint them, or cover them with plastic laminate. Attach the legs to the drawer frame using 2″ screws. Drill pilot holes before installing the screws. Drive the screws through the front and sides into the legs.

With the legs installed, open the door below and push the table back into the opening until the legs hit the bottom of the cabinet. Mark the location of the legs, then pull the table out. Use a sabre saw to cut out the notches for the legs in the

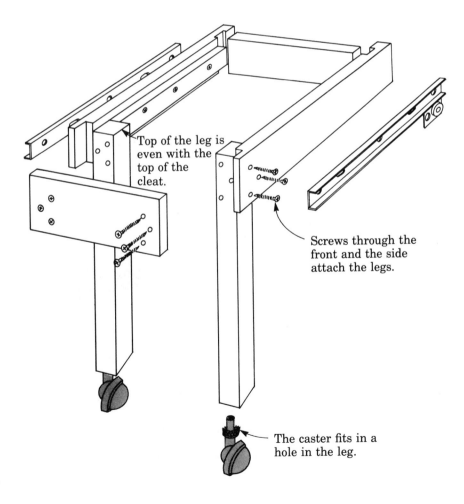

Top of the leg is even with the top of the cleat.

Screws through the front and the side attach the legs.

The caster fits in a hole in the leg.

Illus. 68. The legs attach to the door frame using screws through the side and front. A caster allows the leg to roll as the drawer is opened and closed. The top of the leg should be even with the top of the support cleat.

Illus. 69. Drill a hole in the bottom of the leg for the caster. Drive the sleeve into the hole, then insert the stem of the caster until it locks in place.

Illus. 70. The shelves inside the cabinet must be notched for the legs. Cut as much of the notch as you can with a standard sabre saw blade.

Illus. 71. Switch to a flush-cutting blade to complete the cut close to the side of the cabinet.

Illus. 72. To square-up the corner, place a standard blade in the saw with the blade facing backwards. Position the blade along the straight part of the cut, then pull the saw into the corner.

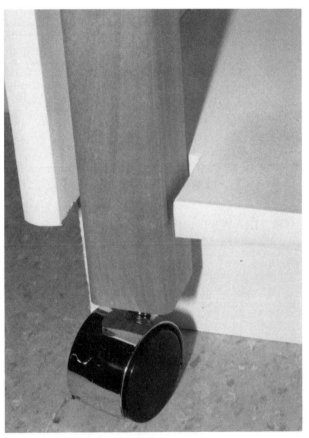

Illus. 73. With the notches complete, test the operation of the hideaway table. The legs should roll smoothly into the notches and not interfere with the door.

cabinet bottom. Cut as much as you can using a standard sabre saw blade (Illus. 70), then switch to a flush-cutting blade to get close to the side (Illus. 71). To square-up the corner, mount a standard blade in the saw facing backwards as shown (Illus. 72). You may need to finish the cut next to the bulkhead with a handsaw. Slide the table back into the drawer opening and the legs should fit into the notches and allow the door to close (Illus. 73).

Project 7
Hideaway Table

BILL OF MATERIALS

Note: 1. Dimensions allow for ½″ clearance on sides for drawer guide.
2. Leg length is oversize. Cut to final dimension after trial assembly with casters.

6″ × 15″ DRAWER OPENING

Part	Description	Size	No. Req'd
A	sides	¾ × 4 × 22	2
B	front & back	¾ × 4 × 13¼	2
C	cleats	¾ × 2½ × 17¼	2
D	false front	¾ × 6 × 15	1
E	cutting board	1½ × 18⅝ × 12⅜	1
F	legs	1½ × 1½ × 33	2

6″ × 18″ DRAWER OPENING

Part	Description	Size	No. Req'd
A	sides	¾ × 4 × 22	2
B	front & back	¾ × 4 × 16¼	2
C	cleats	¾ × 2½ × 17¼	2
D	false front	¾ × 6 × 18	1
E	cutting board	1½ × 18⅝ × 15⅜	1
F	legs	1½ × 1½ × 33	2

PROJECT 8—DROP LEAF COUNTER EXTENSION

When you have a counter that has a free end that is not butted against a wall, you can add temporary work space with a drop leaf extension. The extension folds down when not in use (Illus. 74).

Illus. 74. A drop leaf counter extension folds down out of the way when not in use.

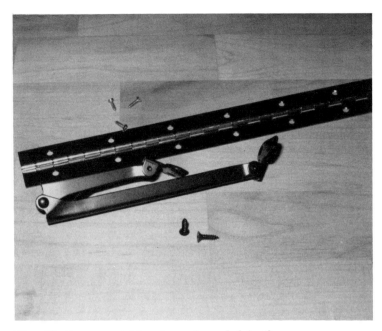

Illus. 75. Some special hardware is needed for the drop leaf. A continuous piano hinge attaches the drop leaf to the cabinet. Two drop leaf supports are used to lock the drop leaf in the "up" position.

Buy the drop leaf hardware before beginning the project. You will need two drop leaf supports and a continuous piano hinge that is as long as the width of the counter. Both items can be found at most home center stores (Illus. 75).

The counter extension can be made from plywood or particleboard and covered with plastic laminate, or you can make a cutting board that is the appropriate size. For a plastic laminate-covered counter, begin by cutting a piece of particleboard or plywood to the desired size. Fir plywood doesn't make a good substrate for plastic laminate because of variations in the gráin. If you want to use plywood, use birch. Particleboard makes a good substrate for plastic laminate. Cut 2″ wide strips of the same material, use glue and nails to attach them to the bottom of the board. Make sure that the strips are flush with the edges of the board. This thickens the edges to match the 1½″ thickness of most counters. Install

Illus. 76. With a hacksaw, cut the piano hinge to the exact length required.

edging that matches the existing counter. Cut the laminate for the top allowing a ½″ overhang. Use contact cement to glue the plastic laminate to the top. Apply the cement to both surfaces and let it dry. A piece of laminate this large may be hard to position accurately. You can make the job easier by placing scrap strips of laminate on top of the board. These strips must not have any contact cement on them. Position the plastic laminate on the top. The strips will separate the glue surfaces so they won't stick together as you position the laminate. When the laminate is positioned correctly, pull out one of the strips and press the laminate down; then remove the rest of the strips, pressing the laminate into place. Roll down the laminate and trim as described in project 3.

If you want to make a cutting board, follow the directions in projects 4 or 12. Make the cutting board 1½″ thick.

The piano hinge is attached with screws to the underside of the counter and to the extension. You can cut the hinge to the exact length required using a hacksaw (Illus. 76).

Proper placement of the drop leaf supports is vital. Follow the directions that come with the drop leaf supports, and attach them to the underside of the extension and to the end of the cabinet (Illus. 77).

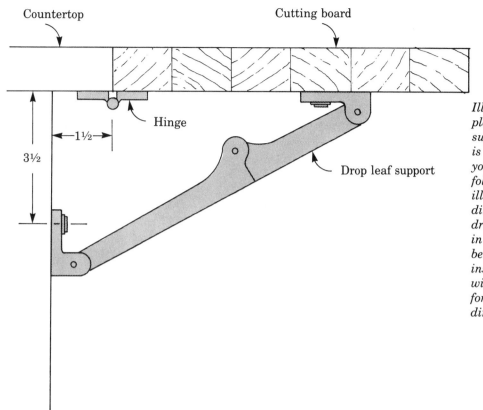

Illus. 77. Proper placement of the drop leaf support is important. If it is not properly placed, you will have trouble folding it down. This illustration gives the dimensions used with the drop leaf support shown in the illustrations, but be sure to check the instructions that come with the drop leaf support for the proper dimensions.

PROJECT 9—COUNTERTOP INSERT

A countertop insert can be used to add a cutting board or heat-resistant surface to a plastic laminate countertop (Illus. 78). You will need a sink rim to install the insert. Buy the sink rim first, because it will determine the size and shape of the insert.

For a cutting board insert, glue some hardwood strips as described in project 4. You can omit the dovetail cleat, because the sink rim will keep the board flat and allows for dimensional change. Cut the board to fit inside the rim. The board can be made flush with the surface of the countertop, or it can be raised. To raise the cutting surface, use a router to

Illus. 78. A countertop insert can be used to add a cutting board or heat-resistant surface to a plastic laminate-covered countertop.

Illus. 79. Mark the location of the cutout by holding the rim in position and tracing around the tail on the rim.

cut a cove around the edge of the board. A special edge-coving bit that has a pilot to guide the cut will follow around the curved corners of the board.

For a heat-resistant insert, use ceramic tile or stainless steel. In either case, start with a piece of ½″ plywood cut to fit into the sink rim. Stainless steel can be purchased from a metal fabricating company, and they will be able to cut it to shape for you. The steel is placed in the rim first and backed up with the plywood. The ceramic tile must be glued to the plywood using mastic. Follow the directions that come with the mastic. Nip off the corners on the tile to fit in the sink

Illus. 80. Use a sabre saw to cut out the opening. Masking tape applied to the countertop will keep the saw from scuffing the surface.

Illus. 81. The insert is held in place with clips that come with the rim. Hook the clip into the tail of the rim, then tighten the screw.

rim. Let the mastic set for the amount of time called for in the directions, then fill the spaces between the tiles with grout.

To cut the hole for the insert, place the rim in position on the countertop and trace around the outside edge of the tail on the rim (Illus. 79). If you have a damaged spot on the countertop where it has been burned or scratched, you can place the insert so that the damaged section is removed. Use a sabre saw with a fine-tooth blade to cut the opening. To protect the adjacent surfaces, put some 2″ wide masking tape on the counter around the cutting line. Drill an entrance hole for the blade inside the waste area. Put the blade in the hole and turn on the saw. Guide it around the cutting line. Cut right on the line; this will give you just enough clearance to install the insert easily (Illus. 80).

Before installing the rim, apply caulk to the rim around both the inside and the outside lips. This will keep spilled liquids from getting under the rim. Put the sink rim into the hole and install the insert. Use the clips and screws that

Illus. 82. This island is made from ready-made base cabinet modules. Plywood and mouldings are used to cover the sides and back.

come with the rim to attach the insert to the countertop (Illus. 81). Any caulk that squeezes out from under the rim can be removed with a damp rag.

PROJECT 10—BASE CABINET ISLAND

A base cabinet island can be a simple yet impressive addition to your kitchen. The unit is constructed from prefabricated base cabinet modules, so you don't need a lot of cabinetmaking skills (Illus. 82). Decide on the size of island that you want, then go to a cabinet showroom and order the required modules. You can also order a prefabricated countertop at the same time.

Assemble the cabinet modules together with face frame screws. Use screws through the face frame and bulkheads to rigidly attach the modules into a single unit (Illus. 83).

The ends and back of the unit should be covered with ¼" plywood that is finished to match the cabinets. You can usually order the caps from the cabinet company. You can make them yourself using plywood with a hardwood face veneer. You can also use the prefinished wood panelling to make the caps. Apply the caps to the cabinets using panelling adhesive and prefinished panelling nails. Use mouldings to hide any joints in the caps.

The countertop attaches to cleats built into the top of the cabinet modules. Apply panelling adhesive to the cleats and

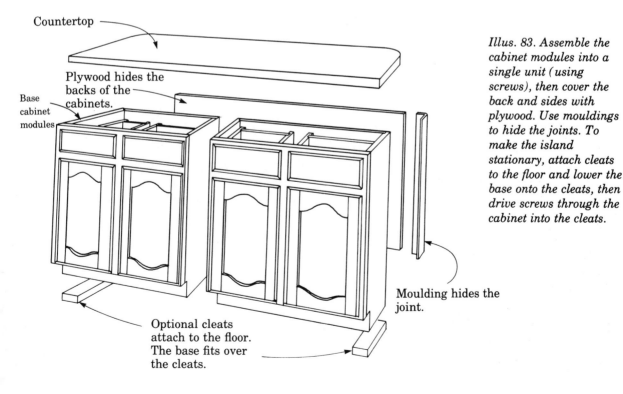

Countertop

Plywood hides the backs of the cabinets.

Base cabinet modules

Optional cleats attach to the floor. The base fits over the cleats.

Moulding hides the joint.

Illus. 83. Assemble the cabinet modules into a single unit (using screws), then cover the back and sides with plywood. Use mouldings to hide the joints. To make the island stationary, attach cleats to the floor and lower the base onto the cleats, then drive screws through the cabinet into the cleats.

set the counter in place. Have someone press down on the counter while you install a few screws through the cleats into the underside of the counter. Be sure that the screws are the proper length so that they won't cause a bulge in the countertop or break through the surface. The screws should be about ¼" shorter than the combined thickness of the cleat and the top.

The island doesn't need to be attached to the floor. The weight of the cabinet will keep it from sliding around, but you can still move it when necessary to mop the floor or to change the arrangement of the room. If you install plumbing

Illus. 84. This movable island is made with overhead cabinet modules. Casters attach to cleats on the bottom of the island.

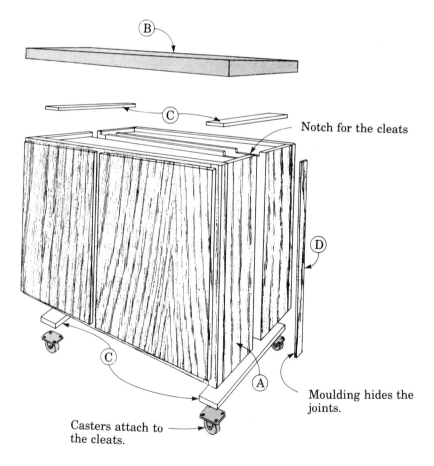

Notch for the cleats

Moulding hides the joints.

Casters attach to the cleats.

or electrical wiring in the island, then it's best to attach the unit to the floor using screws. An easy way to attach the unit is to cut two cleats from 2 × 4s to fit inside the base. Mark the location of the island on the floor, then move the island out of the way. Screw the cleats down to the floor, set back from the marks by the thickness of the cabinet sides. Lower the island onto the cleats. Drive screws through the sides into the cleats.

PROJECT 11—MOVABLE ISLAND

This island has casters for complete mobility. You can move it next to the wall when you want added floor space, or you can push it into the center of the work area when you need it. Prefabricated cabinet modules are used, but instead of base units, overhead cabinets are used. The overhead modules are 30″ high; with the addition of the casters and the top, the overall height comes to the standard 36″ (Illus. 84).

Purchase two 12″ × 36″ × 30″ overhead cabinet modules. Get the modules that have finished sides, or get end-caps for them. You can order a countertop, or make the butcher block top in project 13. You will also need one 8′ length of 1 × 6 and four 4″ casters.

Put the two cabinets back-to-back and measure the distance between the back of the face frame to the same spot on the opposite cabinet. Use this measurement to cut four lengths of 1 × 6. These are the cleats that hold the unit together and provide a strong attachment point both for the casters and for the countertop.

The backs of the cabinets may project past the top and bottom self of the cabinet. The top and bottom shelves are usually set back from the ends of the sides by about ¾ inch. The back is usually cut the full dimension of the sides. This leaves ¾ inch of the back extending past the outside face of the shelf. The projecting part of the back must be trimmed away where the cleats will attach. Mark the location of the cleats, and then use a coping saw or a sabre saw to cut away the projecting portion of the back. Next, place the modules back-to-back. Apply panelling adhesive to the cleats and put them in place. Drive several screws through the cleats into the top of the cabinet. For added strength, you can drive screws from inside the cabinet through the top and into the cleat. This is needed especially when the cabinet top is made of particleboard. The screws will hold much better when driven into the 1×6. Turn the unit over and attach the cleats to the bottom of the cabinets.

Position the casters and mark the hole locations. Drill ¼″ diameter holes through both the cleat and the cabinet bottom. Bolt the casters to the bottom using carriage bolts. Install the bolts so that the round head is inside the cabinet and the threaded end is projecting from the bottom. Use a lock washer between the nut and the caster. Use bolts that are close to the exact length so that the bolts won't project greatly past the nut. If the bolts are too long, they will interfere with the operation of the casters.

Cover the joint between the two cabinets with a piece of pre-finished moulding. Apply panelling adhesive to the top cleats and set the countertop in place. Drive screws from the inside of the cabinet through the cleat and then into the top.

PROJECT 12—BUTCHER BLOCK COUNTERTOP

A butcher block countertop is ideal for an island. It provides a large surface that can be used to chop vegetables, carve meat, cut out cookies, etc. If the surface becomes too scarred

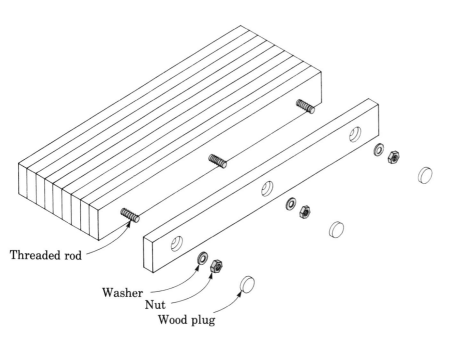

Threaded rod

Washer
Nut
Wood plug

Illus. 85. This butcher block countertop is assembled using threaded rod. Drill the holes in all the pieces before assembly. Insert the threaded rod as you glue the boards. Tighten the nuts to clamp the joints.

by cuts and gouges, you can sand it smooth using a belt sander.

Because of its large size, constructing a butcher block counter is different from constructing a cutting board. Threaded rod is used both to help hold the boards together and to allow for some freedom of movement (Illus. 85). Hardwood is best for a butcher block, but hardwood can be expensive for a project of this size. If you don't mind sacrificing some durability, you can use fir 2×2s to build the butcher block. Select straight, clear lumber for the top. It may be difficult to find good quality fir 2×2s. You may have better luck getting good 2×6s and then cutting them in thirds. You can use short lengths of wood joined end-to-end with dowel joints to make the length you need. Make sure that you stagger the joints in adjacent boards.

You will need three lengths of ⅜″ threaded rod and nuts and washers. Longer countertops require more rods; space them about 12″ apart. Drill the holes for the rods in each board before assembly. Use a ½″ diameter drill bit to allow for a bit of clearance around the ⅜″ diameter rod. The first and last boards both have a recess for a plug to hide the nuts. Make the recess by drilling halfway through the board with a 1″ diameter bit. Continue the hole all the way through, using a ½″ bit. The rods should be cut so that the ends will be recessed about ½″. Use a hacksaw to cut the rod to the desired length. Thread a nut onto the rod before making the cut. When you remove the nut after making the cut, the nut will straighten out any damaged threads.

Begin assembly by first putting the rods into the first board and then by installing the washers and nuts. Apply glue to the next board and then slide it onto the rods. Continue to apply glue and to slide the boards on until all of the boards are on the rods. Work fast so that the glue on the first boards doesn't dry before you are finished.

Install the washers and nuts and run them up "finger tight," meaning as tight as you can turn the nut by hand without using a wrench. Place the block faceup on two sawhorses. Place a block of wood on top of the block and hammer down any misaligned boards. Tighten the nuts with a deep socket wrench. Stop tightening when all of the joints have closed up and a small amount of glue is squeezed out.

When the glue sets, scrape off the excess and sand the top smooth with a belt sander. Cut some ½″ thick wood discs to plug the recesses in the sides where the nuts are. Apply glue to the edges of the discs and drive them into the holes. Sand the discs flush when the glue is dry.

Finish all surfaces with a nontoxic penetrating oil. Use products called either salad bowl finish or butcher block finish.

If any of the joints should separate later, chop out the plugs, retighten the nuts, and then install new plugs. If you used dry lumber, you usually won't need to retighten the nuts.

PROJECT 13—STOWAWAY ISLAND

When floor space in your kitchen is limited, a stowaway island may be what you need. It tucks away under the countertop or in an unused corner when not in use, so it doesn't use up valuable floor space (Illus. 86).

The bill of materials lists dimensions to fit several standard cabinet openings. If you will be storing the island next to a cabinet, make it 36″ high to match the existing counter. The islands that are stored inside a cabinet must be shorter to fit under the existing counter.

The island can be made to fit behind an existing door, or you can attach the door to the front of the unit. The same basic island is used in both cases (Illus. 87). Cleats attached

Illus. 86. A stowaway island (for storage) fits under the counter or in an unused corner of the kitchen.

Illus. 87. Construction of the stowaway island is simplified by the use of metal leg-attaching plates and screws hidden with dowel buttons.

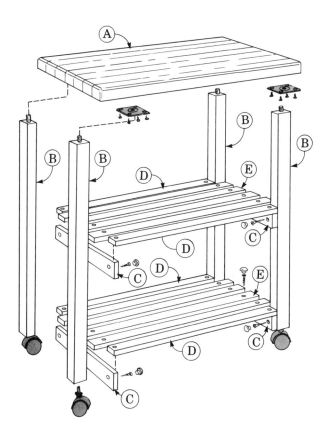

to the front legs are used to attach the door, if desired.

Begin construction by making a butcher block countertop (Part A). Follow the directions in project 12. The legs are 1½″ square. Glue two ¾″ thick boards together, if necessary, to get this dimension. The legs (Part B) are attached to the underside of the butcher block with commercial leg-attachment plates. You can purchase these plates at most home center stores. A lag screw with machine threads on one end is driven into the end of the leg. Drill a pilot hole in the leg for the lag. Put two nuts on the machine threads. Use a wrench on the top nut to install the lags. The nuts will jam

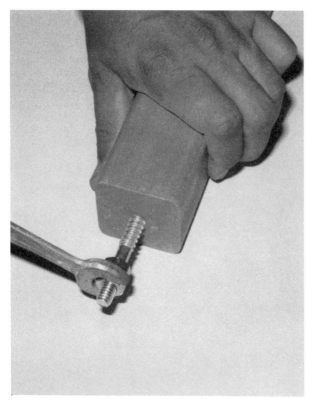

Illus. 88. A lag screw with machine threads on one end attaches the leg to the metal plate. Drill a pilot hole for the lag screw in the end of the leg. Put two nuts on the machine thread end. Place a wrench on the top nut and screw the lag into the leg.

Illus. 89. Attach the leg-mounting plate to the underside of the butcher block using screws.

together so you can turn the lag with the wrench (Illus. 88). Attach the leg-mounting plate to the underside of the butcher block with screws (Illus. 89). Screw the end of the lags (in the legs) into the plates.

Attach the cleats (Part C) to the legs. The bottom of the lower cleats should be flush with the end of the leg. The center cleat can be placed wherever you want, depending upon the height of the objects you will store on the shelf. The cleat is attached with a 1¼" long no. 8 screw. The screw head is set below the surface and hidden by a dowel button (Illus. 90). You can purchase the dowel buttons at most hardware or home center stores. For added strength, apply some glue to

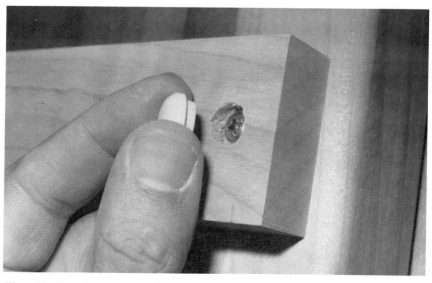

Illus. 90. Dowel buttons can be used to conceal the screws that hold the cleats and shelf slats in place. Countersink the screw below the surface, then glue the dowel button in the hole.

the back of the cleat where it meets the leg. After the screws are tightened, apply some glue to the dowel button and glue it in place.

Install the four short slats (Part D). They fit between the legs, the outside edge is flush with the outside edge of the leg. The rest of the slats are evenly spaced between the short slats. They overhang the cleat, and the ends are flush with the outside edge of the legs. Use 1″ long no. 8 screws to secure the slats to the cleat. Set the heads below the surface and hide them with dowel buttons. Before installation, apply glue to the bottom of the slat where it contacts the cleat. When the screws are tight, glue the dowel buttons in place.

Drill holes in the center of the ends of the legs for the casters. Drive the mounting sleeve into the hole (Illus. 91). The shaft on the caster fits into the sleeve and locks in place.

Finish the island as desired. Use a nontoxic finish on the food preparation area.

Next, prepare the cabinets where you'll store the island. If you add the stowaway island at the same time as you install

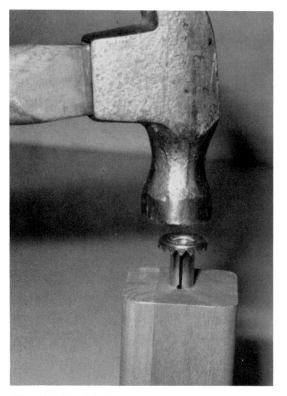

Illus. 91. Drill holes in the ends of the legs for the casters. Drive the mounting sleeve into the hole, then push the stem on the caster into the sleeve until it locks.

Illus. 92. If you removed a drawer to make the opening for the stowaway island, attach the drawer front to the door using a cleat across the back. This will make a larger door to conceal the island, and the door will match the surrounding cabinets.

new cabinets, just omit one of the cabinet modules and replace it with a stowaway island. When adding to an existing cabinet, remove the door and the drawer and cut out the interior shelves. If the flooring doesn't continue under the cabinet, add a piece of hardboard to bring the floor inside the cabinet flush with the level of the finished floor. Use a piece of aluminum trim to cover the joint. This allows the casters to roll smoothly into the cabinet. You can reuse the existing door front. If you removed a drawer to make the opening, remove the drawer front and attach it to the door, using a cleat across the joint in the back. Drive screws through the cleat into the door and the drawer front. This creates a larger door that will match the surrounding cabinets (Illus. 92).

I prefer to have the door hinged to the cabinets, because you can then close the door while the island is in use. But, if you prefer, you can mount the door to the front of the island. You can then pull the island out by using the door pull. There are two advantages to this: the island is easy to pull out, and the island can be used when partially extended from the cabinet. The disadvantage is that should you move the island to another location, you will leave be an uncovered hole in the cabinets. If you place the island *next to* a cabinet instead of placing it below the counter, you'll avoid this disadvantage, and the attached door will make the island blend in with the rest of the cabinets. To attach the door, make two cleats that fit across the front legs. Use screws to attach the cleats near the top and the bottom of the legs on the outside. Put the door in place, and then drive screws through the cleats into the back of the door.

Project 13
Stowaway Island

BILL OF MATERIALS

Note: Leg length is oversize; adjust dimension to suit counter height and caster size.

15″ × 22″

Part	Description	Size	No. Req'd
A	butcher block top	1½ × 15 × 22	1
B	legs	1½ × 1½ × 34	4
C	cleats	¾ × 1½ × 14	4
D	edge slats	½ × 1½ × 18	4
E	center slats	½ × 1½ × 21	10

casters (4), leg attaching plates (4), 1½″ no. 8 wood screws (36), dowel buttons (36)

18″ × 22″

Part	Description	Size	No. Req'd
A	butcher block top	1½ × 18 × 22	1
B	legs	1½ × 1½ × 34	4
C	cleats	¾ × 1½ × 17	4
D	edge slats	½ × 1½ × 18	4
E	center slats	½ × 1½ × 21	14

casters (4), leg attaching plates (4), 1½″ no. 8 wood screws (44), dowel buttons (44)

15″ × 24″

Part	Description	Size	No. Req'd
A	butcher block top	1½ × 15 × 24	1
B	legs	1½ × 1½ × 34	4
C	cleats	¾ × 1½ × 14	4
D	edge slats	½ × 1½ × 20	4
E	center slats	½ × 1½ × 23	10

casters (4), leg attaching plates (4), 1½″ no. 8 wood screws (36), dowel buttons (36)

18″ × 24″

Part	Description	Size	No. Req'd
A	butcher block top	1½ × 18 × 24	1
B	legs	1½ × 1½ × 34	4
C	cleats	¾ × 1½ × 17	4
D	edge slats	½ × 1½ × 20	4
E	center slats	½ × 1½ × 23	14

casters (4), leg attaching plates (4), 1½″ no. 8 wood screws (44), dowel buttons (44)

2
STORAGE SPACE

If you need additional storage space in a small kitchen, you need to use existing space more efficiently. There are several areas in a kitchen that can be used for storage. The projects in this chapter use space that is normally wasted. The Hoosier cabinet made efficient use of every inch of available storage space. One example is the use of racks on the back of the doors (Illus. 93, 94).

The most useful cupboard space is the first three or four inches on the shelf, where everything is in easy reach. You can double the amount of this useful space by using the *door* for storage space. The space available is just the right size for spices, small utensils, glasses and cups.

The simplest way to add door storage is to hang a rack on the back of the door, as was done in the Hoosier cabinet (Illus. 95). The rack is an easy project to build, and can be attached to the door using screws. See project 14. If the rack hits the shelves when you shut the door, then cut back the shelves.

Illus. 93. The Hoosier cabinet made efficient use of space by including racks on the back of the door for spices and other items. This is now a popular accessory for modern built-in cabinets.

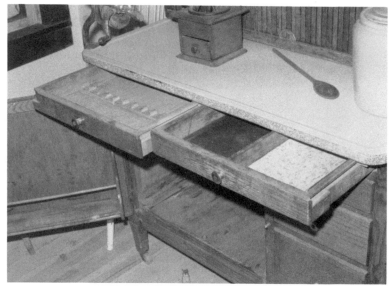

Illus. 94. A large door rack on the lower door of the Hoosier cabinet was used to store canned goods. Notice how the dowel across the front kept things from falling off the shelf as the door opened.

Door-in-Door Storage

Another way to use the door as storage space is the *door-in-door* concept (Illus. 96). The insert door is hinged on the side opposite to the main door, so pulling one handle opens the main door, and pulling the other handle opens the insert door. The insert door can be mounted three different ways. The insert door can be flush with the main door (Illus. 97); the insert door can have a lip that overhangs the opening and hides the gap between the doors (Illus. 98); or a full overlay door can be used (Illus. 99). A box mounted on the back of the main door houses the small shelves (Illus. 100). See project 15.

Pull-down Racks

The area just below an overhead cabinet is a convenient eye level storage space that usually goes to waste (Illus. 107).

Racks mounted under the cabinets can be used to store spices, utensils, cutlery or cookbooks (Illus. 102, 103). Special hardware makes the rack swing down and out for easy access (Illus. 104). You can buy ready-made pull-down racks, or you can make your own customized racks. The procedures for making any of the racks are basically the same, but different dividers are used depending upon the items to be stored. See project 16.

Illus. 95. This is a modern adaptation of the kind of rack used in the Hoosier cabinet. It attaches to the back of a cabinet door. See project 14.

Dummy Drawer Storage

The area immediately below a sink or a built-in cook top is usually wasted, because a full-size drawer won't fit there. A dummy drawer front is used to close off the area (Illus. 105). With the addition of a tilt-out tray, you can use these dummy drawers as storage areas for small items (Illus. 106). First, remove the dummy drawer fronts. They are usually held in place with cleats attached from the rear. You can buy stainless steel or plastic trays to attach to the back of the drawer front. Attach the drawer front to the cabinet using hinges on the bottom of the drawer front, or use special tilt-out hardware. The tray will tip out when you pull on the handle. See project 17.

Illus. 96. The door-in-door concept gives you access to a door-mounted rack from the front.

Drawers

Drawers can make use of hard-to-use space. The space below a drop-in range is often wasted; adding a drawer can give you a useful storage space for pots and pans (Illus. 107).

The space below the base cabinets is called the toe-kick. With the addition of a drawer, it can also be used as storage space (Illus. 108). This drawer is a good place to store garbage bags and similar items. Since toe-kick drawers are in

Illus. 97. This door-in-door rack uses a flush-mounted door. Notice that there is a visible gap around the inner door.

Illus. 98. A lipped door hides the gap between the insert door and the large door.

easy reach of toddlers, they can also be used as storage space for children's toys and games. **Don't use this type of drawer to store anything that would be dangerous to children.**

It is easiest to install a toe-kick drawer when installing new cabinets. A shallow drawer is constructed to fit between the base cabinet supports. Mount the drawer on roller guides. Use a recessed pull so you won't stub your toes on it. See project 18.

Stud-space Cabinets

A standard interior wall is hollow. Use this hollow space by recessing a shallow cabinet into the space between the studs (Illus. 109). Don't use an exterior wall, because you will disturb both the insulation and the vapor barrier. Most interior

Illus. 99. A full overlay door also hides the gap, but it projects farther from the surface than a lipped door.

walls are framed with 2×4 studs spaced 16" on center. This means that there is a space 14½" wide and 3½" deep between the studs. The plaster and lath or drywall adds another ⅜" to 1" to the depth available. You can increase the depth by having the cabinet project slightly from the wall. The available depth is just right for a spice rack, or for a single row of cans or glasses. See project 10.

If you can use the space between the existing studs, you won't need to modify the wall framing. Use an electronic stud finder to find the stud locations. Stud finders are inexpensive, and you will find the stud locations without damaging the wall.

If you want a larger opening, or if the existing cavity is not in the right location, the work becomes more complicated. Virtually anyone can install a cabinet in an existing stud cavity; but if you need to change the framing, it is good to have some carpentry experience. Unless you are confident in your knowledge of carpentry, don't cut the studs in a bearing wall. A bearing wall carries structural loads. A bearing wall usually runs perpendicular to the floor joists. A nonbearing wall usually runs parallel to the joists.

Build the cabinet to fit the space. The cabinet can be used to store small canned goods, appliances, or built-in accessories such as a fold-down ironing board (Illus. 110).

Illus. 100. When the main door is open, you can see the small box that houses the insert rack.

Pantries

A pantry gives you a large storage space for kitchen supplies. The "traditional" pantry is a small room located off the kitchen. Most homes can't afford the space for a full-fledged pantry, but a smaller version can be squeezed into the kitchen. If there is a closet close to the kitchen, you can modify it to serve as a pantry. Add shelves and racks to make

Illus. 101. The area just below the overhead cabinets is a convenient eye-level storage space that usually goes to waste.

Illus. 102. A pull-down rack can be used to store frequently used cookbooks. In the pulled-down position, the rack holds the book open at eye level.

efficient use of the space. A large variety of wire racks and baskets can be added to a closet to make it into a pantry (Illus. 111). See project 20.

When a closet isn't available, you can make a large free-standing cabinet (Illus. 112). The cabinet can be placed in any unused area of the kitchen. The space next to the refrigerator is often a good location. The cabinet can simply be a large box, and you can divide up the space inside with commercial wire shelves and racks. See project 21.

The deep shelves in a pantry can be inefficient, since most of the storage area is hidden behind the first row of items. *Pantry racks* can help to make the storage more efficient (Illus. 113). The racks (holding a single row of canned goods) are hinged; they can be opened to reveal the rest of the storage space behind them. Like the door racks in project 14, they increase the available space that is within easy reach. See project 22. The pantry racks can be installed in an existing cabinet, or a special pantry cabinet can be made. See project 21.

If you do a major kitchen remodelling, consider adding a pantry in a corner. Corner cabinets and counter space are the

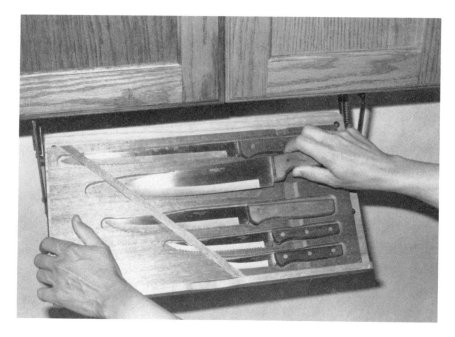

Illus. 103. Pull-down racks also make a convenient storage area for frequently used cutlery or utensils.

least useful areas in a kitchen because they are hard to reach into. Put the space to better use as a walk-in pantry (Illus. 114). Build the pantry using standard framing practices. Fill the interior space with wire shelves and racks.

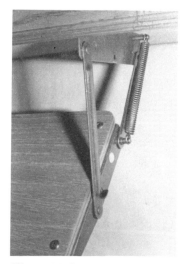

Illus. 104. Special hardware is the secret behind the pull-down rack.

Illus. 105. Dummy drawer fronts are usually used in front of a sink or cook top because there is not enough room for a standard drawer.

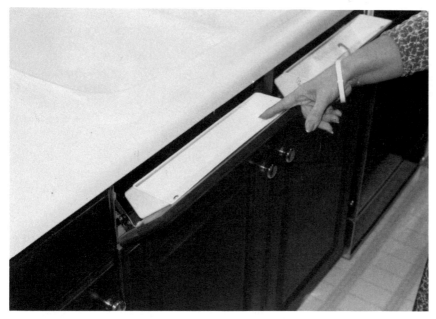

Illus. 106. Tilt-out trays mounted behind dummy drawer fronts make use of this space.

Illus. 107. This drawer, below a drop-in range, can be used to store pots and pans.

Illus. 109. Unused wall space can be converted to a useful storage area with the addition of a stud-space cabinet.

Illus. 108. A toe-kick drawer can be used to store such items as extra plastic wrap or paper bags. Because it is low to the ground, it also makes a good place for toddlers to keep toys or treats.

Illus. 110. The stud-space cabinet can be used for accessories such as a built-in ironing board.

Illus. 111. A standard closet can be turned into a pantry with the addition of wire racks, bins, or shelves.

Illus. 112. A large freestanding cabinet can be built to match the kitchen cabinetry. To use the cabinet as a pantry, place wire racks inside.

Illus. 113. Hinged pantry racks make items more accessible.

Illus. 114. When you're planning a major kitchen remodelling, you can build a pantry into a corner between two sets of cabinets.

Projects

PROJECT 14—DOOR RACK

A rack on the back of a door can be used as a spice rack or a storage for other small items. This rack is made from 1 × 4 lumber because it is widely available; if you find some ½″ thick lumber, you can use it to gain some additional space. The size of the rack depends upon the size of the door. Be sure to make the rack smaller than the door opening so that it will clear the frame as it opens. The most clearance is needed on the side opposite the hinge. If the shelves are full width, you will need to cut them back to accommodate the rack.

Begin construction by cutting the sides (Part A) to length (Illus. 115), then set the dado blade in a table saw to make a ¾″ wide dado. The top and bottom of the rack are set in 1″.

The rest of the shelves can be placed to suit the items you want to store. Make the dadoes in the sides, then drill the holes for the dowels. The holes are blind; they don't go all the way through the board.

Next, cut the shelves (Part B) to length, and cut the dowels to length (Part C). Apply glue to the joints and assemble. Use finish nails to reinforce the joints.

Cut the attaching cleats (Part D) to fit between the sides of the assembled shelf. Use glue and finish nails to attach the cleats. Finish the rack to match the cabinets, then attach it with screws through the cleats to the back of the door.

Project 14
Door Rack

BILL OF MATERIALS

Fits 15″ × 30″ door

Part	Description	Size	No. Req'd
A	sides	¾ × 3½ × 28	2
B	shelves	¾ × 3½ × 11¼	5
C	dowels	⅜ dia. × 11¼	4
D	cleats	¾ × 1 × 10½	2

Fits 18″ × 30″ door

Part	Description	Size	No. Req'd
A	sides	¾ × 3½ × 28	2
B	shelves	¾ × 3½ × 28	5
C	dowels	⅜ dia. × 13¼	4
D	cleats	¾ × 1 × 12½	2

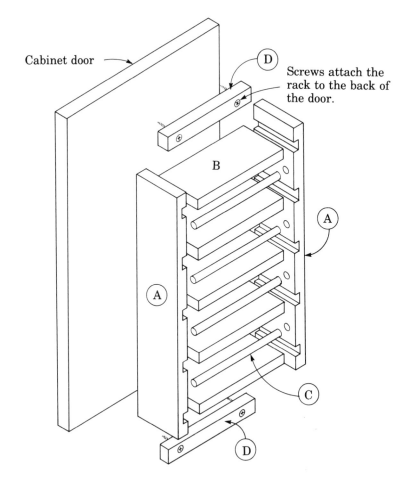

Cabinet door

D

Screws attach the
rack to the back of
the door.

B

A

A

C

D

PROJECT 15—DOOR-IN-DOOR RACK

The door-in-door rack makes a perfect spice rack. It can also
hold cups or glasses. Replace the existing door with a new
unit consisting of a box with shelves, a face frame, and a
smaller door (Illus. 116). The shelves inside the original cabinet may need to be cut back if they interfere with the new
unit. Make sure that there will be enough clearance between
the box and the face frame of the cabinet so that the box won't

hit the frame as the door is opened. You may want to make a full-size drawing of the opening and make a paper cutout of the new unit to test the clearance. Place the cutout on the drawing and put a pin at the hinge pivot point. Move the cutout as if you were opening the door, and see if the box hits the face frame. If more clearance is needed, make the new face frame wider and the box smaller.

Make the face frame first. It should have the same outside dimensions as the original door. The frame is made from 2″ wide lumber. Drill blind dowel holes to reinforce the joints. Apply glue to the joints and insert the dowels. Assemble the face frame, use bar clamps to hold the joints tight until the glue sets.

Next, build the box. The box is made of ½″ thick plywood. Use a hardwood plywood that matches the rest of the cabinets. Cut a rabbet at each end of the sides (Part D), then cut the dadoes for the shelves. The face veneer of plywood tends to splinter when you cut a dado. You can prevent this by applying masking tape over the area where the joint will be cut.

The top and bottom (Part E) are cut to the same width as the sides; the shelves (Part F) are ¼″ narrower than the sides. This allows for the thickness of the shelf rails that hide the plywood edges and keep things from falling off the shelf.

Assemble the box using glue and finish nails. Position the box on the back of the face frame and make sure that it is square with the opening. Rack the box to align with the opening if necessary. Apply bar clamps to hold the box in position as the glue sets.

After removing the clamps, install the shelf rails. They are cut from ¾″ thick solid lumber. Set the table saw to rip ¼″ thick strips from the edge of the board. Sand the strips to remove the saw marks, then cut to length. Spread glue on the front of each shelf and place the rail so that ¼″ is projecting above the top of the shelf. Use a few small brads to hold the rail in place as the glue sets.

Attach the box to the face frame, driving screws through the face frame into the sides of the box. The door will cover the screw heads; they will only be visible when the door is open. If you want a concealed attachment, use blind dowels. Drill the dowel holes in the sides, then use dowel centers to mark the location on the face frame. Dowel centers are metal plugs that fit into the dowel hole. They have a small point in the center. With the dowel centers in the holes, place the box on the face frame in the correct position. Tap the back of the box with a mallet near each dowel location. The points on the dowel centers will leave a mark on the face frame. Drill holes in the face frame for the dowels. Stop drilling before the drill breaks through the front of the board. Spread glue on the front of the box and drip some glue into the dowel holes and insert the dowels. Put the box in position on the face frame and clamp until the glue dries.

Cut a back from ¼″ plywood (Part H). Spread glue on the back of the box and attach the back using small brads.

Illus. 116. Project 15 plans.

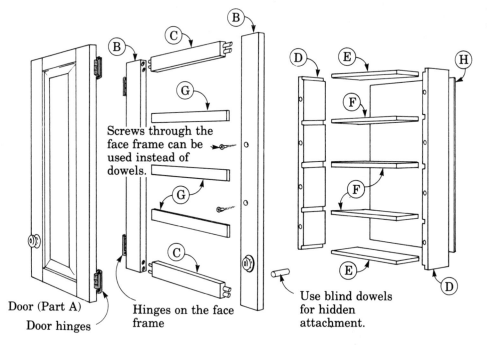

Screws through the face frame can be used instead of dowels.

Door (Part A)
Door hinges

Hinges on the face frame

Use blind dowels for hidden attachment.

The small door should match the existing cabinets. With some styles, you may be able to cut down the original door. If you can't cut down the door, you will need to make a new door or order one from a cabinet manufacturer. Finish the door and the rest of the unit to match the rest of the cabinet. Attach the small door to the face frame with the hinges opposite the hinges that attach the face frame to the cabinet (Illus. 117). Install pulls on both the face frame and the small door, then place the unit in the cabinet and attach the hinges.

Project 15
Door-in-Door Rack

BILL OF MATERIALS

Fits 15″ × 30″ door opening

Part	Description	Size	No. Req'd
A	inner door	¾ × 12 × 27	1
B	stiles	¾ × 2 × 30	2
C	rails	¾ × 2 × 11	1
D	sides	½ × 4 × 27	2
E	top and bottom	½ × 4 × 11½	2
F	shelves	½ × 3¾ × 11½	3
G	shelf rails	¼ × ¾ × 11	3
H	back	¼ × 12 × 27	1

Fits 18″ × 30″ door opening

Part	Description	Size	No. Req'd
A	inner door	¾ × 15 × 27	1
B	stiles	¾ × 2 × 30	2
C	rails	¾ × 2 × 14	1
D	sides	½ × 4 × 27	2
E	top and bottom	½ × 4 × 14½	2
F	shelves	½ × 3¾ × 14½	3
G	shelf rails	¼ × ¾ × 14	3
H	back	¼ × 15 × 27	1

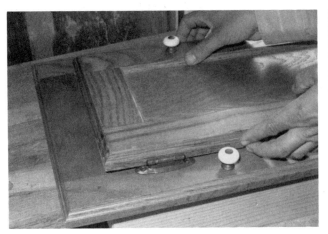

Illus. 117. Attach the insert door to the main door, placing the hinges on the opposite side.

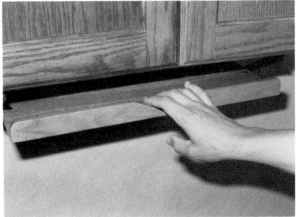

Illus. 118. Pull-down racks fold up out of sight when not in use.

PROJECT 16—PULL-DOWN RACKS

A pull-down rack makes use of the waste space below overhead cabinets. When not in use, the racks fold up out of sight (Illus. 118). The basic rack is simply a shelf with a rail across the front. The addition of dividers or special holders can make a variety of specialized racks (Illus. 119).

The basic rack is made from ½" plywood. Use a hardwood plywood that matches the cabinets. Cut the plywood to size and round off the rear corners. Make the front rail from ½" thick hardwood. Cut out the finger pull using a sabre saw and then sand the edges. Apply glue to the front edge of the plywood and attach the rail with a few small brads.

You can make a spice rack that is designed to fit the small rectangular tins of spices. After cutting out the plywood, cut the ¼" wide dadoes for the dividers. Rip the dividers from the edge of ¾" thick solid lumber. This will give you a divider ¼" thick and ¾" wide. Glue the dividers into the dadoes. The spice rack has rails on all four sides. Rip the rails from ½" thick solid lumber. Attach the rails using glue and brads.

Illus. 119. Project 16 plans.

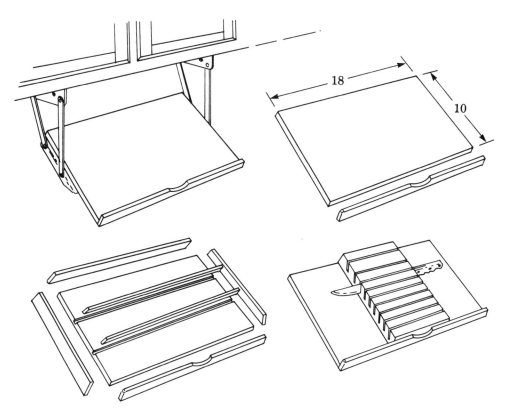

There are two types of knife racks. Make the first type by cutting a series of saw kerfs in a block of wood. The knives will rest in the grooves. Attach the block to the rack using screws driven from the underside.

The second type of rack has routed pockets that are custom-made for a particular set of knives (Illus. 120). To make this rack, start with a piece of solid hardwood. Lay out the knife set on the board and trace around each knife. Before routing the openings, make two dadoes. The first dado serves as a finger space to get a grip on the knife handles. Make it ¾″ wide and ¼″ deep; place it so that it crosses all of the handles about in the center. The second dado is cut on an angle; use a mitre gauge to guide the cut. Set the angle so that the dado crosses all of the blades about 1″ in from the tip. After the

Illus. 120. Use a router to cut out the openings in the knife rack.

Illus. 121. Using short screws, attach the pull-down hardware to the underside of the cabinet. Make sure that the screws don't break through the surface of the shelf inside the cabinet.

openings have been routed, glue a strip of wood into this dado to hold the knives in place.

To rout the openings, put a core box bit in the router. Clamp the board to the bench and rout out the openings. Work freehand for this operation; getting the *exact* shape of the opening isn't necessary.

Use your imagination to come up with a number of other uses for pull-down racks. A phone center, for example, is simply the basic rack with a note pad, phone number file, and a small one-piece telephone attached.

Once you have made the wood parts, install the hardware. Use a special type of hardware made specifically for pull-down racks. If you can't find this hardware at a local home center store, try one of the mail order woodworking supply companies. You can also buy the complete racks ready-made. If you like, you can buy a ready-made cookbook rack and then add your own custom dividers.

Attach the racks to the bottom of the cabinets using screws. The hardware may come with a paper template. This template makes positioning the screw holes easy. Tape the template to the cabinet and push the point of an awl through the marks. Remove the template and drill pilot holes, taking care not to drill all the way through the bottom shelf; then hold the rack in place and install the screws (Illus. 121).

PROJECT 17—TILT-OUT TRAYS

A normal drawer can't be used underneath a sink or cook top. Usually the drawer opening is closed off with a dummy drawer front. Tilt-out trays are used to make use of the wasted space behind such a dummy drawer front. Remove the dummy drawer front and add a tilt-out tray under the sink to add storage space for small items such as scrub brushes. Use the trays as a spice rack under the cook top (Illus. 122).

These trays are available in either plastic or stainless steel. Some trays come with special hardware that is completely concealed when the tray is closed (Illus. 123). Other trays use standard hinges mounted on the lower edge of the drawer front.

To add tilt-out trays, first remove the dummy drawer front. It is usually attached with cleats inside the cabinet (Illus. 124). It may also be attached with screws or staples. After removing the cleats, the drawer front will come off. Remove all staples or other fasteners from the drawer front and from the cabinet face frame and sand down any rough places. If the inside of the drawer front or the face frame isn't finished, apply a finish that matches the rest of the cabinet.

Illus. 122. Tilt-out trays can be used in front of a sink or, as shown here, in front of a cook top. Tilt-out trays in front of a cook top can be used to store frequently used spices. These trays are made of stainless steel. Plastic trays are also available.

Illus. 123. This tilt-out tray uses special hardware that is completely concealed when closed. Other types use standard hinges on the bottom edge of the drawer front.

Attach the hinges and the tray to the drawer front. Put the assembly in place on the cabinet and install the rest of the screws in the hinges. If the tray has an adjustable stop, bend it to rest against the inside of the face frame when the tray is opened correctly.

Illus. 124. To add a tilt-out tray to an existing cabinet, remove the cleats that hold the dummy drawer front in place. The drawer front is reused when the trays are installed.

PROJECT 18—TOE-KICK DRAWER

A toe-kick drawer utilizes the space below the bottom shelf of a base cabinet. This space is usually closed off by a board called the toe-kick. Because the drawer is close to the floor, it isn't a convenient spot for items you use frequently; but it is a good place to store such items as extra garbage bags. The location on the floor makes this an ideal drawer to give to a small child as a personal storage space for toys.

Installing the drawers is easiest when you are installing new cabinets. It is difficult to get into the back of the opening to attach the drawer guides if you install them in existing cabinets, but it can be done. Remove the toe-kick board from the front of the cabinet. This reveals the opening available for a drawer. Measure the inside dimensions of the opening and build a drawer to fit. Remember to allow for the side clearance required by the drawer guides. Usually the side

Illus. 125. Project 18 plans.

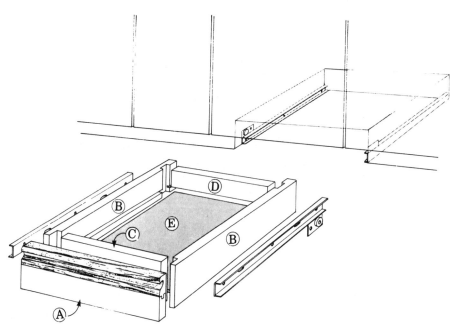

guides need ½″ clearance on each side, so make the drawer 1″ smaller than the opening.

Use ½″ lumber or plywood to make the drawer parts (Illus. 125). Cut the sides (Part B) first. Set the dado blade on the table saw to make the rabbets on the front of the drawer, then reset the saw to make the dadoes for the back. Cut the front (Part C) and the back (Part D) to size. Set the table saw to cut a ⅛″ groove ¼″ away from the bottom edges of the sides and the front. The back is not as wide as the front, so no groove is needed in the back. Cut the bottom using ⅛″ thick hardboard, then begin assembly.

Apply glue to the joints and place the front into the rabbet of one side. Make sure that the grooves for the bottom line up. Use finish nails driven through the side to secure the joint. Next place the back into the dado on the same side. Align the back so that the bottom is flush with the top edge of the groove for the bottom in the side. Secure the joint with nails. Attach the other side. Slide the bottom into the groove. Place the drawer on the bench with the bottom up. Make sure that the drawer is square, then nail small box nails through the bottom and into the back (Part D). Box nails have heads that hold the bottom on better than finish nails will (Illus. 126).

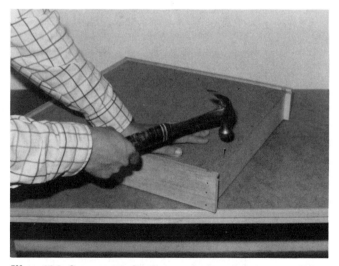

Illus. 126. Square-up the drawer frame, then use small box nails to nail the bottom to the back.

Make a false front (Part A) to match the rest of the cabinets. Use a recessed pull. The type shown in the plan is a continuous oak pull that is glued into a groove on the top of the drawer front.

Attach the drawer guides according to the manufacturer's instructions (Illus. 127). Slide the drawer into the opening and the drawer is ready to use.

Project 18
Toe-kick Drawer

BILL OF MATERIALS

Note: Dimensions allow ½" clearance on side for drawer guides.
Fits 4" × 15" opening

Part	Description	Size	No. Req'd
A	false front	¾ × 3⅞ × 14⅞	1
B	sides	½ × 3½ × 18	2
C	front	½ × 3½ × 13½	1
D	back	½ × 3⅛ × 13½	1
E	bottom	⅛ × 13½ × 17¼	1

Fits 4" × 18" opening

Part	Description	Size	No. Req'd
A	false front	¾ × 3⅞ × 17⅞	1
B	sides	½ × 3½ × 18	2
C	front	½ × 3½ × 16½	1
D	back	½ × 3⅛ × 16½	1
E	bottom	⅛ × 16½ × 17¼	1

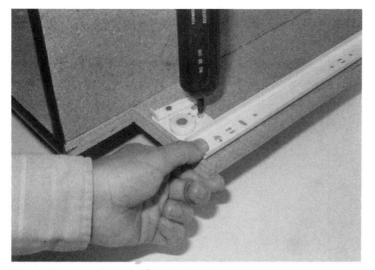

Illus. 127. Attach drawer guides to the sides of the cabinet. This is easiest to do before the cabinet is installed, but it can be done in an existing cabinet.

PROJECT 19—STUD-SPACE CABINET

A stud-space cabinet makes use of the space inside a wall. Use it to store items such as spices or canned goods (Illus. 128).

Pick the approximate location for the cabinet. Avoid areas close to electrical outlets or plumbing, because you may run into electrical wires or pipes inside the stud cavity. Use an electronic stud finder to locate the studs in the area (Illus. 129).

If the existing stud cavities are in a suitable location, the next step is to determine if there is any plumbing or electrical wiring in the wall. Some electronic stud finders can be used to find metal pipes and wires. You can also get a good idea of what may be inside the wall by the proximity of nearby electrical outlets, switches or plumbing fixtures. If you suspect that there is electrical wiring nearby, turn off the circuit breaker or remove the fuse before cutting into the wall. Make a small inspection hole first and use a mirror to check inside the stud cavity for pipes or electrical wires. If

Illus. 128. Project 19 plans.

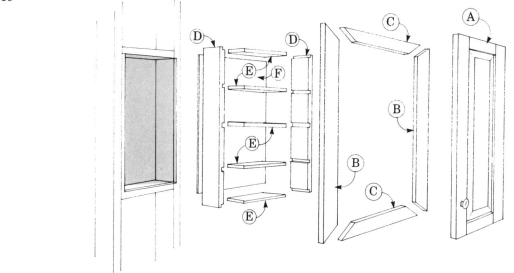

the cavity is clear, use a drywall saw to cut out the opening.

The vertical studs on either side of the opening serve to box off the sides of the opening, but you will need to add 2×4s to the top and bottom of the opening. Cut two pieces of 2×4 to fit between the studs. Next drive a nail into each of the existing studs for the blocking to rest on. These nails should be $1\frac{1}{2}''$ past the edge of the opening in the center of the stud. Drive the nail halfway in so that half of it is still projecting to catch the blocking. Slip the blocking into the opening and slide it behind the drywall until it is stopped by the nails (Illus. 130). Use angled nails to toenail into the studs, then drive a few drywall nails or screws through the drywall into the blocking. When the opening is complete, build the cabinet to fit the opening.

Begin construction of the cabinet by ripping the sides (Part D) and shelves (Part E) to width. The width of these parts is equal to the depth of the opening minus $\frac{1}{4}''$ (for the back).

Cut the rabbets and dadoes in the sides, then assemble the cabinet using glue and nails. Before the glue has a chance to set, slide the unit into the opening in the wall. If it needs to be racked slightly to fit in the opening, do it now. Remove the unit and attach the ¼″ plywood back using glue and nails.

The face frame is made from ¾″ thick × 2″ wide solid lumber. Mitre the corner joints, then attach Parts B and C to the front of the cabinet using glue and finish nails.

Now install the unit in the opening. Slide it in place and drive screws through the sides into the studs to secure it. Build a door or buy one to match the existing cabinets. Attach the door to the face frame using hinges designed for an overlay door.

Illus. 129. Use an electronic stud finder to find the stud locations.

Project 19
Stud-space Cabinet

BILL OF MATERIALS

Fits 14½″ × 30″ opening

Part	Description	Size	No. Req'd
A	door	¾ × 14½ × 30	1
B	stiles	¾ × 2 × 33	2
C	rails	¾ × 2 × 16½	2
D	sides	½ × 3¼ × 30	2
E	shelves	½ × 3¼ × 14	5
F	back	¼ × 14½ × 30	1

Fits 14½″ × 48″ opening

Part	Description	Size	No. Req'd
A	door	¾ × 14½ × 48	1
B	stiles	¾ × 2 × 51	2
C	rails	¾ × 2 × 16½	2
D	sides	½ × 3¼ × 48	2
E	shelves	½ × 3¼ × 14	7
F	back	¼ × 14½ × 48	1

Illus. 130. After cutting the opening, add 2 × 4 blocking at the top and bottom. A nail driven partway into the stud will prevent the blocking from falling into the hole while you toenail it in place.

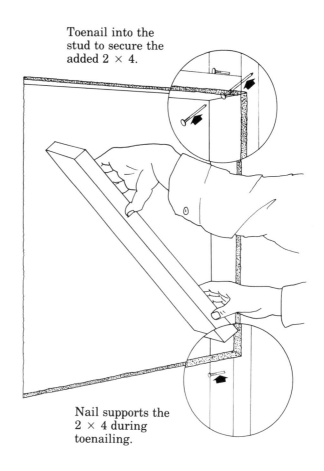

Toenail into the stud to secure the added 2 × 4.

Nail supports the 2 × 4 during toenailing.

PROJECT 20—CLOSET PANTRY

A closet in or near the kitchen can be made into a pantry with the addition of a few shelves, racks or bins. Ready-made wire racks make the conversion easy (Illus. 131).

Plan how you want the space to be divided, then purchase the amount of shelving and brackets that you will need.

Illus. 131. Convert a closet near the kitchen to a pantry by adding wire racks or shelves.

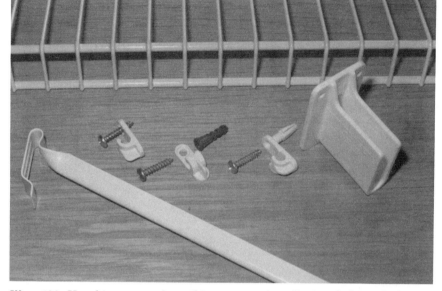

Illus. 132. Use this system of attaching parts to install wire shelving. Left to right: an angle support used to support shelves when they don't meet a sidewall; a clip with a standard screw used when the shelf is attached to a wood cabinet; a mounting clip with a plastic anchor used when the shelf is attached to a masonry wall or a hollow wall; a clip with a built-in anchor; and a plastic "U" bracket used to attach the front of the shelf to a sidewall.

A system of attaching parts is available to install the wire shelves. You can get a variety of wall brackets and supports. Attaching clips are available with a built-in anchor to use in drywall and masonry (Illus. 132). Whenever possible, it's a good idea to drive the screws into a stud. Use an electronic stud finder to locate the studs. Many times there won't be a stud in the right location; in that case, mark the hole locations, then drill a hole through the drywall and insert a plas-

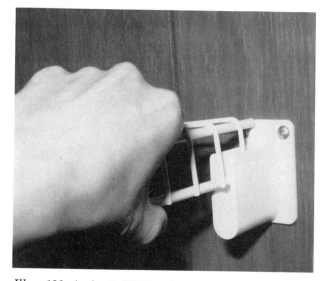

Illus. 133. A plastic "U" bracket attaches to a sidewall to support the front of the shelf.

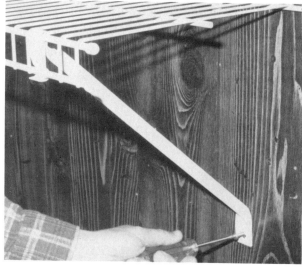

Illus. 134. When the end of the shelf is not next to a sidewall, an angle support is used.

tic screw anchor or one of the clips with the built-in anchor.

The wire shelves can be cut to length using a hacksaw. Draw a level line along the back wall where you want a shelf. Drill holes for at least three clips; long shelves will require more. Install the clips with the open end facing up. Place the shelf in the clips and use a level to position the shelf, then mark the locations for the front supports. When the ends are adjacent to a wall, use a plastic "U" bracket to support the front (Illus. 133). When the end is not next to a wall, use an angle support (Illus. 134). A support pole can be used instead of angle supports when you have multiple shelves (Illus. 135). Some type of shelf support should be used about every 42 inches. When two shelves meet at a corner, you can use a special clip to attach them (Illus. 136). The final step is to install a few clips facing down to hold the shelf in place.

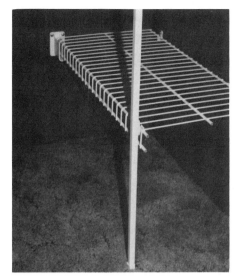

Illus. 135. A support pole can be used when you have multiple shelves.

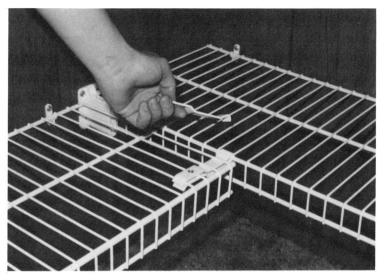

Illus. 136. When two shelves meet at a corner, use a special clip to attach them.

You can add other wire accessories to make the pantry more convenient. Bins and baskets will help organize the area. You can get freestanding bin units that rest on the floor of the closet. A few clips can be attached to the walls to keep the bins from moving, but the legs of the unit provide most of the support. The back of the door can be put to use by attaching small shelf units, racks and hangers.

PROJECT 21—FREESTANDING PANTRY

To add storage space, a freestanding pantry can be placed in an unused part of the kitchen. Make this unit from plywood and stain it to match the other cabinets, or use particleboard and paint it. Basically, it is a large box; you can divide up the space inside by using wire shelves and accessories. Construction is simplified so that you can make this unit with a minimum of equipment (Illus. 137). If you have the lumberyard cut the plywood to size, all you will need is a drill, dowel jig, and a few hand tools. The size of the cabinet is designed to get the maximum use out of 4′ × 8′ plywood sheets (Illus. 138). The depth of the cabinet is 23⅞″; this is about what you will get if you rip a 4 × 8 sheet in half. The sides are 6′ tall, so that the top and bottom can be cut from the leftover pieces.

Begin construction by cutting the parts to size. If you want, you can usually pay a small fee to have the lumberyard do this. Next, use a sabre saw or a handsaw to cut out the toe space at the bottom of the sides.

Blind dowel joints are used to join the top and bottom (Part B) to the sides (Part A). If you use the type of dowelling jig

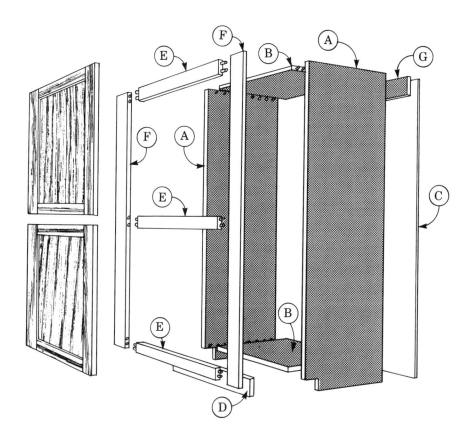

Illus. 137. This freestanding pantry can be built with a minimum of equipment.

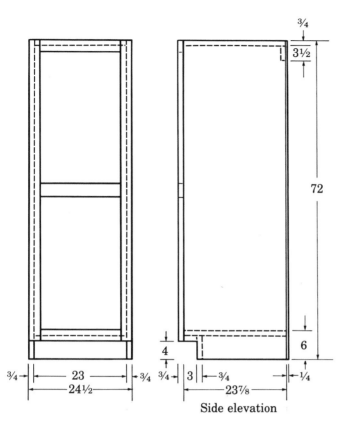

Illus. 138. Project 21 plans.

shown (Illus. 3), you can drill the holes in one part and insert the dowels, then use the dowels to align the jig as you drill the mating holes. Space the dowels about 1¼" on center.

After all of the dowel holes are drilled, apply glue to the joints and dowel holes and assemble. Use bar clamps to hold the joints tight as the glue dries, or drive a few finish nails into the joints. Install the attaching cleat (Part G) using finish nails and glue.

Place the cabinet facedown on the floor and attach the back. The width of the back is ⅝" narrower than the width of the cabinet. This allows you to set the edges back 5⁄16" from the side of the cabinet. By doing this, the plywood edge won't show as much, and you won't need to cut a rabbet for the back. If you have the equipment, you may want to modify the plans to provide a rabbet for the back. Attach the back with small box nails spaced about 1¼" apart.

Turn the cabinet over so it is faceup and attach the toe-kick. The toe-kick is cut from a piece of 1×6 lumber. Apply glue to the joint and attach with finish nails.

The face frame is made from ¾" thick × 2" wide lumber. Lay the pieces on the cabinet and mark the lengths. The stiles (Part F) should extend from the top of the cabinet to the top of the toe space. The rails (Part E) should fit between the stiles. The top rail should be flush with the top of the cabinet on the outside. The bottom rail should be flush with the top of the bottom shelf on the inside. The bottom shelf is positioned above the toe space cutout, so that the bottom of the rail will be flush with the top of the cutout. The center rail is used to allow for standard size cabinet doors. You can omit it if you want to use a single large door.

Use the dowelling jig to drill dowel holes in the joints between the stiles and rails. Apply glue to the joints and dowel holes and insert the dowels. Assemble the face frame and clamp with bar clamps. Place the face frame in position on the cabinet and make it square with the rest of the cabinet. Remove the face frame and apply glue to the front edge of the cabinet. Attach the face frame using finish nails.

Finish the cabinet with stain and varnish, or paint it. Use an oil-based paint. Raw wood will absorb water-based paint, creating a bumpy texture.

Make the doors yourself, or order doors from a cabinet manufacturer to match the existing cabinets. Attach the doors with overlay type hinges.

Divide the interior space using wire shelves, racks or bins, or install swing-out pantry racks. See project 22.

The cabinet can be left freestanding, but drive a few screws through the attaching cleat to make it more stable. If you install swing-out racks that will overbalance the unit when they swing out, then you must attach the cabinet firmly to the wall.

Project 21
Freestanding Pantry

BILL OF MATERIALS

Part	Description	Size	No. Req'd
A	sides	¾ × 23⅞ × 72	2
B	top & bottom	¾ × 23⅞ × 23	2
C	back	¼ × 23⅞ × 72	1
D	toe-kick	¾ × 5¼ × 23	1
E	rails	¾ × 2 × 20½	3
F	stiles	¾ × 2 × 68	2
G	cleat	¾ × 3½ × 23	1

PROJECT 22—SWING-OUT PANTRY RACKS

Make more efficient use of the space in a pantry by adding swing-out pantry racks (Illus. 139). These small shelves on a swing-out unit put everything in easy sight and reach. These racks can be incorporated in the freestanding pantry. See project 21. The racks are hinged to the face frame on the side opposite the door hinges. The width of the unit must be narrower than the door opening because of the large amount of clearance needed for the rear edge of the unit as it swings out. Making the rack too wide can also put too much strain on the hinges. When the racks are opened, they can overbalance a freestanding cabinet, so the cabinet must be firmly attached to a wall.

The shelves of the unit are sized to accommodate most canned goods and items such as cake mixes and pasta.

The sides and shelves are made from ¾″ thick plywood. Rip the sides (Part A) to width and cut to length. Use the dado blade to make the groove for the ¼″ plywood center board (Part B). Reset the dado blade and use it to cut the dadoes for the shelves. Cut out the shelves (Part C), then begin assembly.

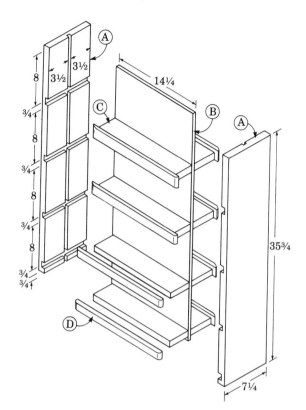

Illus. 139. Project 22 plans.

Start assembly by placing one of the sides on the bench with the dadoes faceup. Apply glue to the groove for the center board and insert Part B. Apply glue to the dadoes and insert the shelves. You may need some help for the next step because there are so many shelves to align. Apply some glue to the groove and dadoes in the second side. Brush the glue evenly inside the joint so the glue won't drip out as you work. Set the side in place, and align the shelves with the dadoes beginning at one end and progressing to the other. When all of the shelves and the center board are in the joints, press the

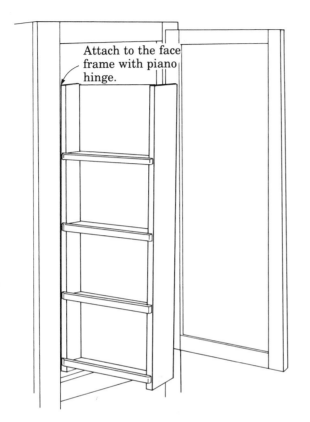

Attach to the face
frame with piano
hinge.

*Illus. 140. The swing-out
pantry rack is attached to
the face frame of the
cabinet using a
continuous piano hinge.
The hinge attaches to the
inside edge of the face
frame and to the side of
the rack. Place the piano
hinge on the side opposite
to the hinges on the
cabinet door.*

side down onto the shelves. Slide the unit to the edge of the
bench and let it overhang the bench. This enables you to
bar-clamp the unit. Use bar clamps on the front and back.
Drive a few finish nails into the joints to reinforce the joints.
Remove the clamps when the glue is set.

Cover the exposed plywood edges on the side and top with
wood veneer tape. Apply the tape using contact cement, or
get heat-sensitive tape that can be applied with a hot iron.
Trim off the excess with a sharp knife or scissors. Sand the
edges of the tape flush with the face of the plywood, then give

it a slight bevel so it won't get caught on something and be pulled off.

A rail on the front of each shelf hides the plywood edge and forms a small lip to keep items on the shelf from falling off. The rail is made by first ripping some ¾" thick lumber into 1" wide strips, and then resawing them to ¼" thickness. Apply the strips to the front of each shelf using glue and small brads. The shelf rails extend all the way to the side of the unit. Round off the corners to keep them from snagging on clothing.

Finish the unit to match the cabinets, then install them using a piano hinge that extends the full height of the rack. The hinge attaches to the side of the swing-out rack and to the edge of a stile on the cabinet (Illus. 140).

Project 22
Swing-out Pantry Racks

BILL OF MATERIALS

Part	Description	Size	No. Req'd
A	sides	¾ × 7¼ × 35¾	2
B	center board	¼ × 14¼ × 35¾	1
C	shelves	¾ × 3½ × 14¼	8
D	rails	¼ × 1 × 15	8

36″ long piano hinge

3
APPLIANCE SPACE

Finding a place to store the many small appliances used in a modern kitchen can be a problem. Appliances should be kept in a convenient location so they will be easy to use, but this often leads to a counter cluttered with small appliances. What you need is a convenient place to hide small appliances. The appliance garage does just that, by serving as a convenient place to park small appliances on the counter. A tambour door (like a rolltop desk) is often used on an appliance garage. The tambour door is another feature that has its origins in the Hoosier cabinet. The tambour door was located at counter level, and it could be opened up when working on the counter, then closed to hide the clutter when not in use (Illus. 141).

The microwave oven is almost standard equipment in today's kitchen. Placing the microwave on a countertop uses much valuable work space. A microwave shelf can open up usable counter space and place the microwave at a convenient working height.

Illus. 141. The Hoosier cabinet used a tambour door to hide the shelf clutter behind the work surface. Modern cabinet designers incorporate the tambour door into appliance garages to hide various small appliances found in modern kitchens.

Illus. 142. An appliance garage is a small cabinet that rests directly on the countertop. Slide small appliances into the garage and they're hidden by the door.

Appliance Garage

The appliance garage is just a small cabinet that sits directly on the counter (Illus. 142). There is no cabinet bottom; the counter serves as the bottom; appliances then slide into the garage. A corner makes a good location for the appliance garage because such a corner isn't an effective work space, anyway. A corner is a central location; appliances from both sides of the counter can be stored in a single convenient location. See project 23.

Standard hinged doors can be used for the appliance garage (Illus. 143). The hinged doors can be made to match the rest of the cabinets, and they are easy to install. The area in front of the garage must be kept clear for the doors to open.

A roll-up tambour door stores out-of-the-way when it is open, and you can open it even if the counter in front of it is in use. You can buy ready-made tambour doors. These doors use a plastic track that attaches to the face frame of the cabinet (Illus. 144). A roller mechanism at the top stores the tambour in window shade fashion. This type of door is easy to install and can be adapted to existing cabinets. If you want to make your own tambour, you can use the more traditional design. See project 24. The traditional tambour is made of wood strips that are tied together with a cloth backing (Illus. 145). The tambour fits into a track cut into the side of the cabinet (Illus. 146).

Illus. 143. Standard hinged doors can be used on an appliance garage. To swing the doors open, you must keep the countertop clear.

Illus. 144. A ready-made tambour door fits into a plastic track that attaches to the face frame of the cabinet.

Illus. 145. A traditional tambour is made from wood strips with a cloth backing glued to them.

Illus. 146. A groove routed into the side of the cabinet serves as a track for the tambour door.

Swing-up Appliance Shelf

Large appliances such as mixers can be stored on swing-up platforms (Illus. 147). These platforms pull up for use and fold down for storage. Since the appliance is stored below the counter, no work space is wasted. Special hardware is needed to make the platform. Make a plywood shelf to fit inside the cabinet, and attach the hardware to the sides of the cabinet. Attach the shelf to the hardware and the platform is ready to use.

Microwave Oven Shelf

A microwave oven shelf provides a place to put the microwave oven above the counter (Illus. 148). The shelf can be built to fit under the overhead cabinets. Make the shelf large enough to allow ventilation to the rear of the microwave oven. See project 25. The shelf will need to carry a considerable weight, so attach the shelf to the wall by driving screws into the studs. Use an electronic stud finder to find the stud locations in the wall. In some cases, the existing cabinets can be modified to accommodate a microwave oven. See Project 26.

The microwave wall unit (Illus. 149) doesn't take up any counter or floor space because it is built into the wall. This design works best when there is a closet behind the wall so that the cabinet can project into the closet. The procedure for cutting the hole in the wall is similar to the one procedure used to make the stud space cabinet, but you can cut all the way through the wall. See project 27. Make sure that the wall

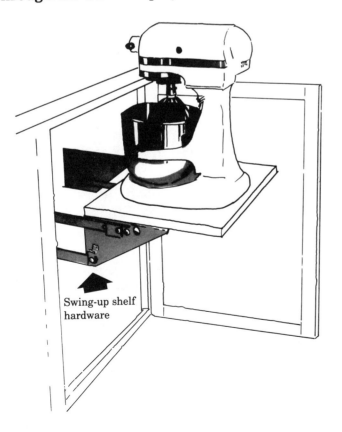

Swing-up shelf hardware

Illus. 147. Large appliances (mixers, etc.) can be stored below the countertop on a swing-up platform. They pull up level with the countertop, ready for use.

Illus. 148. Place a microwave oven on a shelf to free valuable counter space.

Illus. 149. A microwave oven can be placed in a recessed shelf. This works best when there is a closet behind the wall, because the microwave shelf will extend through the back of the wall.

is not load-bearing, because you will need to remove part of one stud to get an area big enough to accommodate a microwave oven. Frame across the top and bottom of the opening with 2×4s. The face frame of the cabinet covers the cutout area on the outside of the wall. To hide the rough edges of the cutout, inside the closet, apply moulding around the cabinet after it is installed.

Projects

PROJECT 23—CORNER APPLIANCE GARAGE

The corner appliance garage is a simple project that will dress up your kitchen and make it more efficient (Illus. 150).

The sides and top of the garage are made of plywood or particleboard matching the existing cabinets. The face frame is made from hardwood lumber that matches, as well. You can use a commercial roll-up tambour door or a hinged door that matches the rest of the doors.

Cut the top (Part B) to width, then cut the ends to 45°. Set the mitre gauge on the table saw to guide the cut, or make a layout line and cut the angle with a handsaw or a portable circular saw. Next, cut the sides (Part A) to size. Notice that the front edges of the sides are cut to 45°. To do this, set the tilt arbor on the table saw to 45° as you rip the boards to width.

The sides are joined to the top using blind dowels. Use a dowel jig and drill the holes 1¼" apart. Apply glue to the joint and insert the dowels. Assemble the joints and drive a few finish nails to hold the joint tight as the glue sets. Because of the angle, it is difficult to use bar clamps on this joint.

The size of the top rail (Part D) shown on the plans is for use with a hinged door; if you use a commercial tambour door, make it so it will hide the tambour mechanism. The edges of the stiles (Part C) are cut to 45°. Join the stiles to the

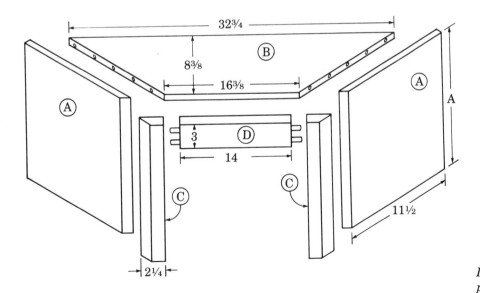

Illus. 150. Project 23 plans.

rail using dowels. Use glue and a few finish nails to attach the face frame to the front of the unit.

If you are using a tambour door, install it before putting the cabinet in position. A hinged door can be attached after the garage is in place.

Attach the appliance garage to the overhead cabinets and to the counter using screws. To find the locations for the screws that go through the counter, slide the garage into its final position and mark the outline on the counter. Slide the garage out again and drill pilot holes down through the countertop. Reposition the garage and drive the screws up from the underside.

To attach the top to the overhead cabinets, drive screws down through the bottom shelf of the overhead cabinet into the top of the appliance garage.

Project 23
Corner Appliance Garage

BILL OF MATERIALS

Note: Dimension A is equal to the distance between the countertop and the overhead cabinets.

Part	Description	Size	No. Req'd
A	sides	¾ × 11½ × A	2
B	top	¾ × 8⅜ × 32¾	1
C	stiles	¾ × 2¼ × A	2
D	rail	¾ × 3 × 14	1

PROJECT 24—TAMBOUR APPLIANCE GARAGE

This tambour appliance garage uses the traditional type of tambour door (Illus. 151). Because the track for the door is cut in the sides, this garage isn't suitable for a diagonal corner application.

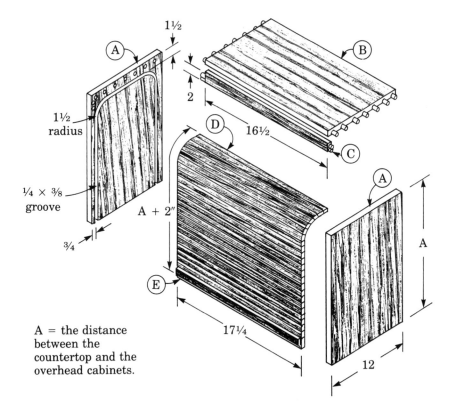

1½

2

1½
radius

16½

¼ × ⅜
groove

A + 2"

¾

A

A

E

17¼

12

A = the distance
between the
countertop and the
overhead cabinets.

Begin by cutting the sides (Part A) from plywood or parti-cleboard that matches the existing cabinets. The height of the sides is equal to the distance between the countertop and the underside of the overhead cabinets.

Next, use a router to cut the groove that serves as the tambour track (Illus. 152). You will need a template made from ¼" hardboard. This template is merely a rectangle with rounded corners. The template size is slightly smaller than the inside measurements of the tambour track. Mount a template-following collar (also called a bushing) on a router and use a straight bit (Illus. 153). Clamp the template to the side of the garage and set the depth of cut on the router to about one-half the thickness of the sides. The collar on the

Illus. 152. A template made from ¼" thick hardboard is used to guide the router while cutting the track for the tambour door.

Clamp holds the template in place.

Template guides the router to make a groove for the tambour door.

router rubs against the template to guide the cut (Illus. 154). Once you have made the track in one side, clamp the template to the opposite side and make the second cut.

Assemble the cabinet before making the door. After the door is finished, you can slide it into the open ends of the track on the bottom of the cabinet. Cut the top (Part B) and the rail (Part C) to size. Drill dowel holes 1¼" apart in the joints using a dowel jig. Apply glue, insert the dowels and assemble. Use bar clamps to hold the joints tight as the glue sets. Cover the exposed plywood edges with wood veneer tape.

To make the tambour door, cut strips of wood to fit inside the track. The strips are ¾" wide and about ¼" thick. Rip these strips from a wide board. Set the rip fence to guide the cut and rip the strips on the table saw.

Make a clamping jig from a piece of scrap plywood (Illus. 155). Make a rabbet in the edges of two boards and nail them to the plywood so that you have just enough clearance to slide in the tambour strips. Nail another board across one end to act as a stop. Slide the tambour strips into the jig face down. When all of the strips are in the jig, use a board to squeeze them tightly together and clamp the board to the jig.

Cut a piece of lightweight canvas to fit on the back of the door, between the boards on the jig. Apply contact cement to the back of the door and to the canvas. When the glue is dry, press the canvas in place on the door. The area under the rabbet in the jig isn't covered with cloth; this is the part of the door that will fit into the track. Leave a flap of canvas about 1″ wide extending from the bottom edge of the door. This flap is used to attach the finger pull to the door.

The finger pull is made of a piece of wood that is ½″ thick and 1″ wide. Make a cove along one edge using a router. Mount the router in a router table and use a coving bit. Set the router fence to help guide the cut. Next, set the table saw to cut a rabbet. Rabbet the ends of the pull so that they fit inside the track; the extra thickness projects from the front of the door; the back of the pull is flush with the rest of the tambour strips. Apply contact cement to the back of the pull and to the flap of canvas. When the glue is dry, attach the pull. Hold the flap back so it won't touch the pull as you position the pull against the bottom edge of the tambour. Press the pull tightly against the strips, then lower the flap

Illus. 153. A template-following collar attaches to the router base. It rubs against the template to guide the cut.

Illus. 154. The template must be slightly smaller than the desired dimension to allow for the thickness of the template-following collar.

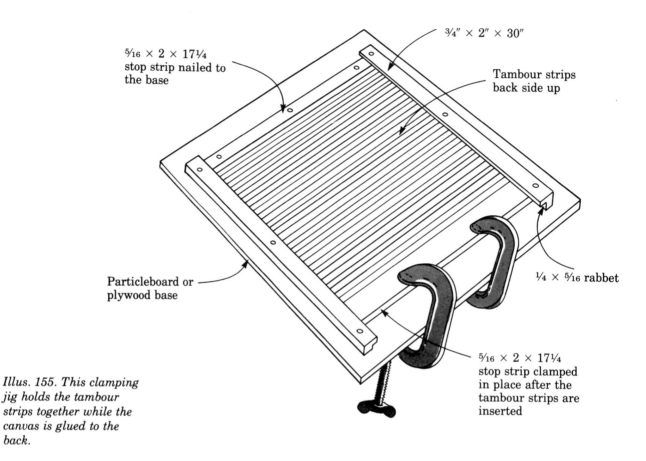

$\frac{5}{16} \times 2 \times 17\frac{1}{4}$ stop strip nailed to the base

$\frac{3}{4}'' \times 2'' \times 30''$

Tambour strips back side up

$\frac{1}{4} \times \frac{5}{16}$ rabbet

Particleboard or plywood base

$\frac{5}{16} \times 2 \times 17\frac{1}{4}$ stop strip clamped in place after the tambour strips are inserted

Illus. 155. This clamping jig holds the tambour strips together while the canvas is glued to the back.

and rub it down on the back of the pull. Trim off any excess canvas that extends past the bottom of the pull. Drive a few staples through the canvas into the pull for added strength.

Stain and varnish the cabinet and the tambour before installing the door. After the finish is dry, slide the tambour into the track from the bottom of the cabinet.

Slide the appliance garage into place on the counter and attach it to the counter and overhead cabinets using screws.

Project 24
Tambour Appliance Garage

BILL OF MATERIALS

Note: Dimension A is equal to the distance between the
countertop and the overhead cabinets.

Part	Description	Size	No. Req'd
A	slides	$3/4 \times 12 \times A$	2
B	top	$3/4 \times 12 \times 16\frac{1}{2}$	1
C	rail	$3/4 \times 2 \times 16\frac{1}{2}$	1
D	tambour strips	$1/4 \times 3/4 \times 17\frac{1}{4}$	varies
E	pull strip	$1/2 \times 1 \times 17\frac{1}{4}$	1

PROJECT 25—MICROWAVE OVEN SHELF

This microwave oven shelf can be hung below overhead cabinets or in any convenient location on a wall. The unit is
made from ¾" thick plywood (Illus. 156).

First, cut the sides (Part A) to size (Illus. 157), then set a
table saw to cut a rabbet for the back. Use a sabre saw to cut
the curve on the sides.

Next, cut the bottom (Part B) and the sides (Part C) to size.
The face rails (Part F) are attached to the front of the shelves
using blind dowels. Drill the holes 2½" on center. Use a dowel
jig to align the holes. Apply glue to the joints, insert the
dowels, and clamp the face rails to the shelves. When the
clamps have been removed, use the dowelling jig to drill the
holes for the dowels that will join the top and bottom to the
sides 1¼" on center. Cut the attaching cleat to length and
drill the dowel holes in the ends and in the sides of the cabinet. Apply glue to the joints and insert the dowels. Lay one
side inside faceup on the work bench. Align the dowels in the
top with the holes in the side and push the joint tight. Install

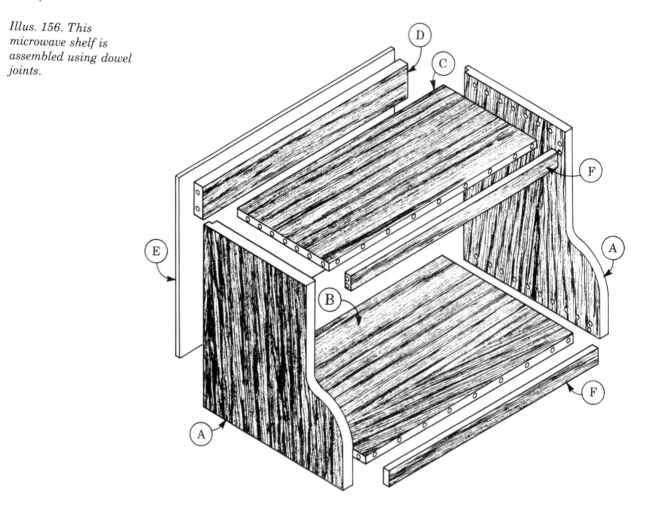

Illus. 156. This microwave shelf is assembled using dowel joints.

the attaching cleat and then the bottom. Put the other side onto the assembly and align the joints. Clamp the cabinet together with bar clamps until the glue is set.

Cover the exposed plywood edges with wood veneer tape. Finish the shelf with stain and varnish to match the existing cabinets, then hang the shelf using screws driven through the attaching cleat into wall studs.

Illus. 157. Project 25 plans.

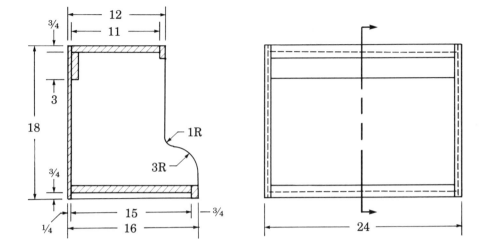

Project 25
Microwave Oven Shelf

BILL OF MATERIALS

Part	Description	Size	No. Req'd
A	sides	$\frac{3}{4} \times 16 \times 18$	2
B	bottom	$\frac{3}{4} \times 15 \times 22\frac{1}{2}$	1
C	top	$\frac{3}{4} \times 11 \times 22\frac{1}{2}$	1
D	cleat	$\frac{3}{4} \times 3 \times 22\frac{1}{2}$	1
E	back	$\frac{1}{4} \times 18 \times 23\frac{1}{4}$	1
F	rails	$\frac{3}{4} \times 1\frac{1}{2} \times 22\frac{1}{2}$	2

PROJECT 26—MICROWAVE SHELF EXTENSION

You can modify an existing cabinet to serve as a microwave shelf (Illus. 158). First, measure the cabinets and find one that is wide enough to accommodate the oven. Remove the

Illus. 158. An existing cabinet can be modified to serve as a microwave shelf.

Illus. 159. First remove the existing cabinet doors.

Illus. 160. A piece of plywood wide enough to fit under the microwave is placed inside the cabinet opening. Drive screws through the shelf to secure it to the cabinet.

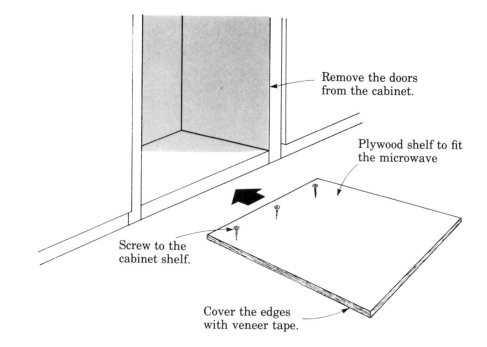

Remove the doors from the cabinet.

Plywood shelf to fit the microwave

Screw to the cabinet shelf.

Cover the edges with veneer tape.

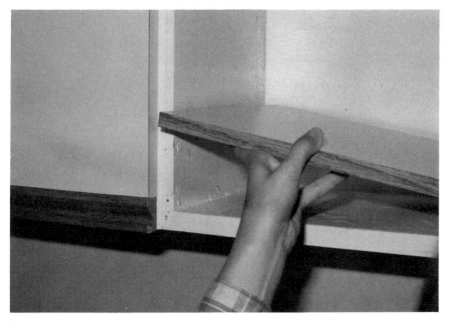

Illus. 161. After applying wood veneer tape to the exposed plywood edges and finishing the shelf to match the existing cabinets, slip the shelf in place and attach it using screws.

screws in the hinges and take off the doors (Illus. 159). Overhead cabinets are usually only 12″ deep. This isn't deep enough for most microwave ovens. Cut a shelf extension from a piece of plywood. The extension should fill the inside of the cabinet and extend out over the edge enough to support the oven (Illus. 160). If the cabinet has a face frame, you may want to cut notches in the sides of the extension shelf to fit around the face frame.

Cover the exposed plywood edges with wood veneer tape. Finish the shelf to match the cabinets. Slide the shelf into place and drive screws down through the shelf into the bottom of the cabinet (Illus. 161). Now you can slide in the microwave oven.

PROJECT 27—MICROWAVE OVEN IN A WALL

Recess a microwave oven shelf into a wall to make use of blank wall space without using up kitchen floor space. This project works best if there is a closet behind the wall space that will be used for the shelf.

The cabinet is made of ¾" thick plywood or particleboard (Illus. 162). The sizes given in the plans will fit in the opening made when you remove one stud, if the studs are spaced 16" on center. Use an electronic stud finder to determine stud spacing and location before beginning construction.

Begin building the unit by cutting the sides (Part A) and

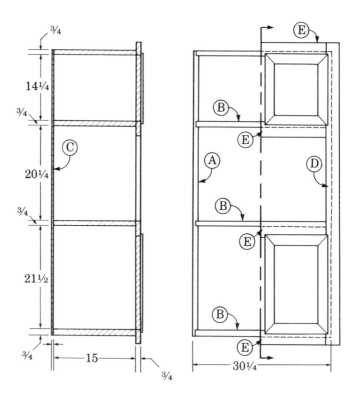

Illus. 162. Project 27 plans.

the shelves (Part B). Next set the table saw to cut a ¾″ wide × ⅜″ deep rabbet on both ends of the sides, then set up the saw to cut a ¾″ wide × ⅜″ deep dado. Cut the dadoes for the shelves in the sides. Attach the shelves to the sides using glue and nails. Square up the unit and attach a ¼″ plywood or hardboard back to it using small box nails.

The face frame is wider than usual because it must cover an exposed 2 × 4 that will be installed in the cutout. Assemble the face frame using blind dowels. Attach the face frame to the front of the cabinet using glue and a few finish nails.

The opening in the wall is wider than a normal stud cavity, so you will need to cut one stud. Make sure that this is not a load-bearing wall. The instructions given here apply only to a nonbearing wall. Consult a carpenter if you suspect that the wall is load-bearing. If your house is a single story with trusses supporting the roof, probably all of the interior partitions are nonbearing. Using an electronic stud finder, find the stud locations. Mark the stud locations and the lines for the top and the bottom of the cut. The opening is 3″ taller than the cabinet to allow for the 2 × 4s that will be used at the top and the bottom of the opening. Use a drywall saw to cut out the opening. Cut through both the front and back sheets of drywall. When you reach the stud that must be cut, switch to a crosscut saw and cut through the stud.

Cut pieces of 2 × 4 to fit across the top and the bottom of the opening. Put the pieces in place and nail through the 2 × 4 into the cutoff stud, then toenail the ends of the 2 × 4 into the studs on either side.

Slide the cabinet into the opening. Drive screws through the sides of the cabinet into the studs to secure it. The wide face frame will hide the exposed 2 × 4s and the rough edges of the cutout on the outside. Inside the closet, install casing moulding around the opening to cover the 2 × 4s and the rough edges.

Add doors to match the other cabinets in the kitchen. Have an electrician add an electrical outlet near the back of the shelf. Now you're ready to slide in the microwave oven and start cooking.

Project 27
Microwave Oven in a Wall

BILL OF MATERIALS

Part	Description	Size	No. Req'd
A	sides	¾ × 15 × 59	2
B	shelves	¾ × 15 × 29½	4
C	back	¼ × 30¼ × 59	1
D	stiles	¾ × 3 × 63½	2
E	rails	¾ × 3 × 28¾	4

4
DISPLAY SPACE

Most kitchen cabinets are designed to hide the clutter inside, but sometimes you want to show off some special items. For these decorative purposes, you need some display space.

Open Shelves

A simple way to get some display space is to remove the doors from a cabinet to create open shelves (Illus. 163). After removing the doors, fill the screw holes with putty and paint or finish to match the rest of the cabinet. You can also build open shelving and add it to the existing cabinets. The space between the end of an overhead cabinet and a window makes a good location for a small display shelf (Illus. 164). See project 28.

Make open shelving more decorative by adding plate racks or glass shelves.

Illus. 163. Display your decorative items. A simple way to create display space is to remove the doors from one cabinet.

Plate Racks

If you have some fine china or decorative plates that you want to display, you need a plate rack. The plate rack is a special type of shelf that holds the plates upright. The shelf has either a groove or a moulding to hold the bottom of the plate so that the plate won't slide out as the plate leans

Illus. 164. A small display shelf can be placed at the end of an overhead cabinet.

Illus. 165. You can add a plate rack to an existing shelf by attaching a piece of moulding.

against the back of the cabinet. The simplest way to add a plate rack to an existing cabinet is to use moulding (Illus. 165). Cove moulding or quarter round can be used. Apply the moulding to the shelf using brads. The exact position of the moulding is best determined by experimenting with the

Illus. 166. Glass shelves clearly make good display shelves.

Illus. 167. A galley rail can be used as a decorative feature along the top of a cabinet.

Illus. 168. The galley rail uses turned spindles that fit into holes drilled into the top and bottom rails.

plates you plan to display. Rest the plate against the back of the cabinet and find the best angle that both shows off the plate and prevents the plate from tipping forward.

If you are making new shelves, or if the existing shelves are the adjustable type that can be removed, you can cut a groove for the plates. Find the location of the groove by experimentation, then set the dado blade on the table saw to make a ⅜″ wide by ¼″ deep cut. Adjust the fence to the correct distance and run the shelf through. See project 29.

Glass Shelves

Glass shelves are good for display, because you can see the bottom of the objects and you can see through the shelves, so the view of one shelf isn't blocked by another one (Illus. 166). The shelves can be purchased from a glass supply store. If you have adjustable shelves, you can simply remove the wood shelf and replace it with a glass one. If the wood shelves are

Illus. 169. Ready-made galley rails are available in a variety of materials. Left: plastic; right: oak.

permanently attached, remove the one you are replacing by cutting it in half with a sabre saw, then install adjustable standards. See project 30.

Galley Rails

The kitchen on a boat is called the galley. Because a boat is constantly rocked by waves, things tend to fall off shelves.

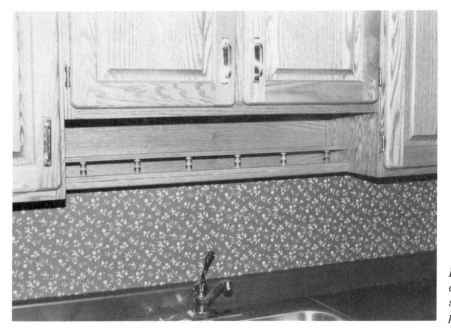

Illus. 170. The galley rail can be used to make a small spice rack. See project 32.

Galley shelves have a rail on the front to prevent things from falling off. Galley rails are used in kitchens more for decoration than for utility (Illus. 167). The rail can be installed across the top of the cabinets as a decoration; the top of the cabinet can then be used as a display shelf. See project 33.

The rail is usually made from two strips separated by turned spindles (Illus. 168). You can buy ready-made spindles in several shapes. You can also buy ready-made galley rails in wood, brass or plastic. This is the easiest way to make the shelf, because the precision work is done for you (Illus. 169).

A galley rail serves a useful purpose when used on a small shelf such as a spice rack (Illus. 170). The rail will hold the spice containers in place on the shelf, as well as adding a decorative touch. See project 32.

Illus. 171. A glazed door allows you to see the contents of a cabinet. The glass protects the contents and keeps out dust.

Glazed Doors

A traditional display space is a cabinet with glazed doors (Illus. 171). If you are installing new cabinets, you can order glazed doors. Existing doors can often be modified to accept a pane of glass or plastic. Panel doors can be modified especially well. The panel must be removed and the frame modified slightly. See project 33.

Solid doors can be modified to accept a pane of glass. You need to consider the strength of the material used to make the door before attempting this. Solid lumber won't work because the grain direction will cause a weakness in the corners. Plywood is the best because it has uniform strength in both directions. Particleboard covered with plastic laminate can be used. It isn't as strong as plywood, but it will hold up under normal use. The center of the door is cut out using a sabre saw, then a router is used to make a rabbet for the glass.

The glass can be held in place in several ways. You can use glazing points and putty. Silicone caulking works well, and it is available in a choice of colors to match the cabinet finish. You can use a wood stop and attach it with brads. Plastic stop can also be purchased. One type is attached with staples; another type has a barbed spline that fits into a groove in the frame. One of the easiest methods is to use metal thumb screws designed just for this purpose.

Projects

PROJECT 28—DISPLAY SHELF

This small display shelf will fit into a corner or on the end of an overhead cabinet. This simple project will add some display space to your kitchen (Illus. 172).

Illus. 172. The shelves and sides are all cut from ¾" thick plywood or particleboard. Dadoes and rabbet joints are used.

All of the parts are cut from ¾" thick plywood or particleboard (Illus. 173). Cut the side (Part A) and back (Part B) first. Set the table saw to cut a ¾" wide × ⅜" deep rabbet, and make rabbets on the top and bottom edges of both parts. Also make a rabbet along the back edge of Part A. Set the saw to make a ¾" wide × ⅜" deep dado and cut the dadoes for the shelves.

The shelves (Part C) are cut as square pieces first, then cut off the front corner at 45°. As an alternate design, use a sabre saw to cut the front of the shelf to a semicircle. Assemble the shelf using glue and nails. Apply wood veneer tape to the edges. Even if you plan to paint the shelf, the veneer will hide the raw edge and make the paint job look better.

Attach the shelf to the cabinet and wall by driving screws through the side and back.

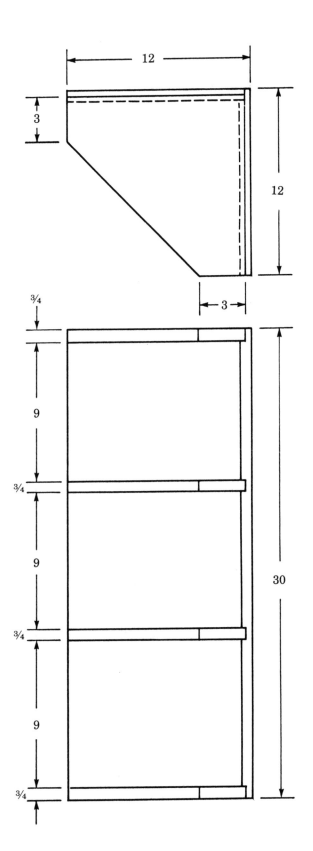

Illus. 173. Project 28 plans.

Project 28
Display Shelf

BILL OF MATERIALS

Part	Description	Size	No. Req'd
A	side	¾ × 11⅝ × 30	1
B	back	¾ × 12 × 30	1
C	shelves	¾ × 11⅝ × 11⅝	4

PROJECT 29—PLATE RACK

You can add a plate rack to a shelf in two ways: either use a moulding, or use a groove to hold the bottom of the plate.

To add a moulding for a plate rack, buy the required length of either cove or quarter round moulding. Cut a piece to fit the shelf. Place the moulding on the shelf and hold one of the plates in position. Hold the moulding down and see if the plate is stable. Adjust the position of the moulding until the plate is almost upright but still leaning against the back of the cabinet with no tendency to tip forward. Mark the location of the moulding and remove the plate. Use small brads to attach the moulding to the shelf (Illus. 174). Either finish the moulding to match the shelf, or to save yourself the bother, use a pre-finished moulding.

If the shelf is the adjustable type that can be removed from the cabinet, you can cut a groove in the shelf to hold the bottom of the plate (Illus. 175). Using a groove is a good method, because you can still use the full width of the shelf for storage where you aren't displaying plates, and less of the bottom edge of the plate is hidden.

Before removing the shelf, experiment with a plate to determine the location of the groove. Remove the shelf and set the dado blade on a table saw to make a ⅜″ wide by ¼″ deep groove. Adjust the fence to guide the cut in the location you

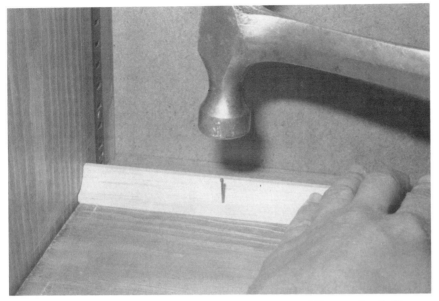

Illus. 174. Use small brads to attach the plate-rack moulding to the shelf.

Illus. 175. A groove, cut using a table saw, can also serve as a plate rack.

have chosen. After cutting the groove, use fine sandpaper to remove any splinters from around the groove. Apply some finish to the groove to match the finish of the shelf, and then reinstall the shelf in the cabinet.

Illus. 176. When adjustable shelves are used, you can easily replace existing shelves with glass shelves.

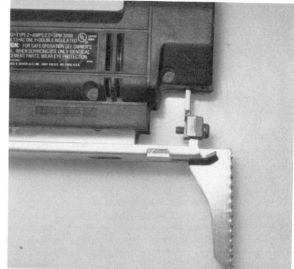

Illus. 177. A flush-cutting sabre saw blade is used to cut the old shelf all the way to the back.

PROJECT 30—GLASS SHELVES

Glass shelves add a nice touch to display spaces. If the existing shelves are the adjustable type, all you need to do is remove the old shelf and replace it with a glass shelf (Illus. 176). The glass shelves can be custom-cut to size at a glass shop. The shop will grind the edges so there are no sharp edges exposed.

If the shelves are not adjustable, you will need to cut them out of the cabinet. Use a sabre saw to cut the shelf in half. You will need to finish the last inch or two with a hand saw, unless you get a special blade for the sabre saw. A flush-cutting blade is offset so that the teeth are in line with the front edge of the base of the saw (Illus. 177). In either case, protect the back of the cabinet from being scratched by the saw. Wedge a piece of cardboard or a scrap of plastic laminate between the shelf and the back of the cabinet. The saw will hit the scrap before it mars the back (Illus. 178).

After the shelf is cut in half, bend it down until it pulls loose from the nails that attach it to the sides of the cabinet.

The nails can be pulled out of the sides using pliers. Grab the nail close to the point where it enters the wood. Place a piece of scrap between the pliers and the side of the cabinet, then bend down on the nail; the lever action of the pliers against the scrap will pull the head of the nail through the side of the cabinet. If you can't get the nail all the way out on the first try, reposition the pliers and start again.

If the shelf is in a dado, cut a strip of wood to fill the dado. If no dado is present, simply remove the nails with a pair of pliers and fill the holes with putty. Paint or stain the area to match the rest of the cabinet interior. Next, install adjustable shelf standards for the glass shelves. The type that fits into holes drilled in the side of the cabinet is less visible than the metal type. If you use this type, drill a series of holes for the clips (Illus. 179). A piece of pegboard makes a good guide for aligning the holes. Place the pegboard so that the same end is always against the bottom shelf as you drill the four rows of holes, and the holes will all line up.

Illus. 178. To keep the saw from marring the back of the cabinet, wedge a piece of plastic laminate between the shelf and the back of the cabinet in line with the cut.

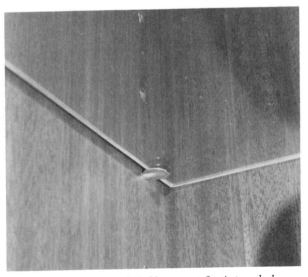

Illus. 179. This type of shelf support fits into a hole drilled into the side of the cabinet.

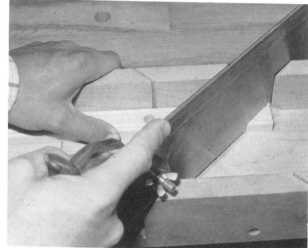

Illus. 180. Instead of using a bottom rail, you can drill holes directly into the top of the cabinet and then place the spindles into the holes.

Illus. 181. Cut the end of the rail at 45° to make a mitre joint where the rails meet. Use a mitre box to guide the cut.

PROJECT 31—GALLEY RAIL

A galley rail can be added to an existing shelf or to the top of a cabinet to make a decorative display area. If you use a manufactured galley rail, then all you need to do is cut it and attach it to the cabinet.

If you prefer to make the rail yourself, lay out the spindle holes with the top and bottom rail side by side. The hole in the bottom rail can go all the way through, but the hole in the top should be blind. Apply glue to the spindles and assemble the railing. When you make your own rail, you don't actually need a bottom rail. The holes can be drilled into the shelf (Illus. 180).

When the rails meet at a corner, use a mitre joint. Cut the ends of the rails to 45° in a mitre box (Illus. 181). Place the rail temporarily on the spindles and drill pilot holes through the corner joint for small brads (Illus. 182). Remove the rail and apply glue to the corner joint, then reinstall the rail and drive small brads into the pilot holes to secure the corner joint. Pre-finish the parts before assembly, then install them on the cabinet.

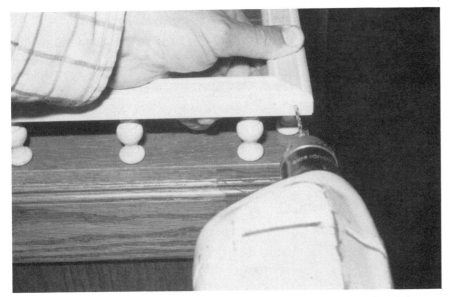

Illus. 182. Drill pilot holes for the small brads used to secure the mitre joint.

To install a manufactured rail, cut the rails to fit the shelf. The corners can be mitred, or you can use special corner spindles. The corner spindles have flats that the rails can butt against so that the ends of the rails can be cut square (Illus. 183). Apply glue to the bottom of the rail and hold it in

Illus. 183. You can buy a special corner spindle for use with commercial galley rails. When this spindle is used, the ends of the rails can be cut square and butted up against the flats on the corner spindle.

place. Drive a few brads through the bottom rail into the shelf. The glue will do most of the holding; the brads just hold the rail in place as the glue dries.

PROJECT 32—GALLEY SHELF SPICE RACK

This spice rack is designed to fit under an overhead cabinet (usually over a sink or stove) that is shorter than the surrounding cabinets (Illus. 184). The shelf is easy to make; it consists of three parts: two boards and a manufactured galley rail. The boards are ¾" thick solid lumber. Cut the two boards to size, then cut a ¾" wide × ⅜" deep rabbet along the back edge of the bottom (Part A). Apply glue to the joint and place the back (Part B) in the rabbet. Drive a few finish nails through the bottom and into the back. Cut the galley rail to

Illus. 184. Project 32 plans.

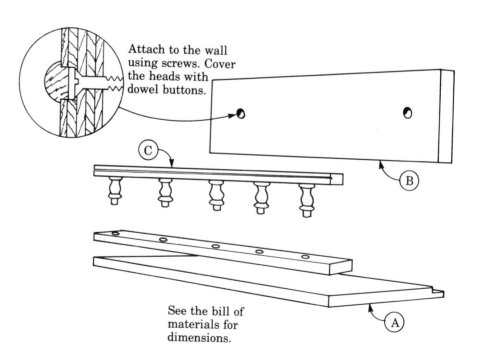

Attach to the wall using screws. Cover the heads with dowel buttons.

See the bill of materials for dimensions.

length and apply glue to the bottom rail. Clamp the rail to the shelf or attach it using a few brads. When the glue is dry, finish the shelf as desired.

Attach the shelf to the wall by driving two screws through the back of the shelf into the wall studs. Countersink the screw holes below the surface and hide the screws using wood dowel buttons. An alternate way to attach the shelf is to apply construction adhesive to the back of the shelf and position the shelf on the wall; drive two finish nails into the wall to hold the shelf as the adhesive sets.

Project 32
Galley Shelf Spice Rack

BILL OF MATERIALS

Note: Dimension A is determined by the space available for the shelf.

Part	Description	Size	No. Req'd
A	shelf	¾ × 4 × A	1
B	back	¾ × 5 × A	1
C	galley rail	length = A	1

PROJECT 33—MODIFYING A CABINET DOOR TO ACCEPT GLAZING

If your kitchen cabinets have panel doors, you can modify one or more of the doors to accept a piece of glass or plastic. This creates a display space that is more protected than open shelves. A plywood door can also be modified to accept a piece of glass or plastic. An otherwise plain-looking set of cabinets becomes something special by adding some display space.

To modify a panel door, first remove the door and all of the hardware. Place the door facedown on a workbench. Place a

Illus. 185. Before using the router to cut away the inside lip on a panel door, remove any staples using a pair of needlenose pliers.

Illus. 186. Use a straight bit in a router to cut away the inside lip that holds the panel in place. Use a board clamped to the door to guide the router.

piece of cardboard between the door and the workbench to protect the finish on the door. Examine the back of the door for nails or staples. There will sometimes be staples in the center of the top and bottom rail securing the panel. Remove any staples by digging around them with a chisel, and then grab them with needlenose pliers (Illus. 185).

Put a straight bit in a router and set the cutting depth to remove the inside lip on the frame that holds the panel in place. Set the router fence to guide the cut along the straight rails, or clamp a board to the door to guide the router (Illus. 186). The board is parallel to the side of the door and offset from the cutting line by the distance between the edge of the bit and the outside of the router base. The router base rubs against the board to keep the cut straight. Clamp the door to the workbench so the door won't move as you work. Make a plunge cut into the back of the door. A plunge cut router makes the job easier, because it allows you to make the entrance cut with the router base flat on the door; but you can also make the cut using a standard router. Hold the router so that the bit is slightly above the wood and the fence is against the edge of the door. Start the router and lower it into the wood. When the router base is resting flat on the door, move the router along the edge using the fence or board to guide the cut. Make all of the straight cuts using the fence or board as a guide. If the door has an arch top, you won't be able to use the fence to cut around the arched area. Cut away as much of the lip as you can by using the fence, then chop away the rest of the lip using a chisel. The panel will now be free. Press on the front to remove it. Using a chisel, square up the round corners left by the router. The door is now ready to accept the glass. Take the door to a glass shop and have the shop cut the glass to fit the opening. Attach thumbscrew glass retainers to the back of the door and put the glass in place. Tighten the thumbscrew finger tight, but don't over-tighten, or you may break the glass. Rehang the door on the cabinet using the original hinges.

To modify the plywood door, first remove the door and take off all the hardware. Mark the outline of the opening. Leave at least 2″ between the new opening and the edge of the door. A wide frame is stronger; 2″ is about right.

Use a sabre saw to cut out the opening. Before you do, apply wide masking tape along the cutting line on the face of the door. This protects the finish and prevents splintering. Drill an entrance hole for the saw blade at each of the corners. Put the blade in the entrance hole and saw over to the line. Once you are on the line, you can attach a fence to the saw to guide the cut straight. When you reach the next corner, stop the saw and lift it from the cut; reinsert it in the entrance hole. If the hole is right in the corner, you should be able to set the saw down without removing the fence. Start the saw and make the next cut. Continue in this way until you have cut all four sides. Use a file to square up the corners.

After the opening is cut, make a rabbet for the glass. Use a router with a rabbeting bit. The bit has a pilot that will ride against the edge of the opening. After routing around the opening, square up the corners using a chisel. The door is now ready to receive the glass.

5

ORGANIZERS

Even when there is plenty of storage space in a kitchen, such space can be hard to use if it isn't well organized. One big problem is that things in the back of cabinets become lost behind other items, and sometimes you remove everything in front just to get at one small item that has been pushed to the back. Modern kitchen designers include pullout shelves to overcome this problem; but as we've seen with other kitchen accessories, the idea can be traced back to the Hoosier cabinet (Illus. 187). The Hoosier cabinet was full of organizers because space was limited and every inch of the cabinet was put to good use. The projects in this chapter are designed to help you organize your kitchen and to get the most benefit from a limited amount of space.

Pullout Shelves

The back of a shelf is often full of things that you don't use because it is too hard to get to them. A pullout shelf makes it

Illus. 187. The Hoosier cabinet incorporated many organizers. These pullout shelves, for example, allow for efficient shelf organization. Items at the rear of the shelf can be easily reached with the shelf in the pulled-out position.

as easy to reach the back of the shelf as the front (Illus. 188).

The heart of the pullout shelf is a metal drawer guide. The guide attaches to the sides of the cabinet and is made so that the shelf can be fully extended and still be supported. You can get special guides made just for use with pullout shelves. These guides fit into an adjustable standard that is mounted to the side of the cabinet. With these standards, the shelves can be adjusted to any height. You can get commercial parts to make the shelf. There are plastic rails that fit around the shelf to keep things from sliding off (Illus. 189). You can even get complete sides with built-in guides so all you need to do is add a bottom of the correct size and mount it in the cabinet. You don't need a lot of fancy hardware; if you want to build the shelves yourself, you can simply build a shallow box around the shelf and add drawer guides. See project 34.

When installing a pullout shelf in an existing cabinet, the first step is to remove the old shelves. Use a sabre saw to cut the shelf in half. It may be necessary to use a handsaw to cut the last inch of the shelf. Bend the shelf down in the center until the two halves separate, and pull out the shelves from the attachment on the sides. If you can't get the shelf to bend down, make an angled relief cut to get more clearance. Remove the nails using a pair of pliers; if there is a dado, fill it with a strip of wood. Now build the new shelves. Be sure to buy the drawer guides first, because they require a side clearance that will affect the size of the shelf. Make the shelf using ½″ or ¾″ thick plywood or particleboard. Build a frame around the edges to prevent things from sliding off as the shelf is moved. Follow the directions that come with the drawer guides for mounting them to the cabinet and to the shelf, then slide the shelf into place.

Illus. 188. This is a modern example of the pullout shelf.

Illus. 189. This pullout shelf uses a commercially available plastic rail to keep items from sliding off while the shelf is pulled out.

Illus. 190. A lazy Susan is a revolving shelf that fits in a corner cabinet. By rotating the shelf, all of the items are within easy reach. This makes efficient use of a space that is usually hard to organize.

Corner Cabinets

Corner cabinets have a lot of interior space, but because of the limited door size, most of the space is inaccessible. Some special hardware can solve the problem.

A lazy Susan (also called a carousel shelf) is a revolving shelf unit that fits into a corner cabinet (Illus. 190). You can buy the hardware with or without shelves. If you make your own plywood shelves, add a strip of metal around the edges to prevent things from falling off as the unit rotates. The metal shelves that can be purchased with the hardware have a lip formed on the edge that serves the same purpose. There are several types of doors that can be used with a lazy Susan. The choice depends on the type of cabinets and how you prefer the doors to open. See project 35.

If you install the type of lazy Susan that is supported by a center pole in an existing cabinet, remove the fixed shelves. You can can get lazy Susan hardware that attaches to the

Illus. 191. Blind-corner shelves come with special hardware that allows them to pivot out of a blind-corner cabinet.

Illus. 192. Storage bins can provide efficient storage for bulk foods. A glass front allows you to see the contents without opening the bin.

existing shelf. This latter method involves fewer modifications to the existing cabinet. See project 36.

Blind-corner shelves make use of the corner space without the need for a special corner door. The shelves are semicircular and pivot out. The wire rack shelf shown (Illus. 191) can be purchased complete with hardware.

Storage Bins

You can save money by purchasing bulk food that is not prepackaged, but how can you store it at home? Storage bins can be the answer (Illus. 192). The bins can pull out like drawers or tilt out for easy access. Large bins can be used for flour and potatoes; smaller bins can handle macaroni, rice and similar items. The front of the bin can be solid, or you can use a glass front so that you can see the contents, or wire mesh to provide ventilation. See project 37. The type of bin

Illus. 193. This pullout garbage bin keeps the garbage hidden, but pulls out for easy access when needed.

that pulls out like a drawer can have adjustable dividers so that you can store several different items in the same bin. See project 38. The space between the countertop and the overhead cabinets can be closed in and filled with bins. A pullout bin isn't a good choice for this application, because everything must be removed from the counter in front of the bin before you can open the bin. In this a tilt-out bin is a better choice. See project 39.

Garbage Containers

The kitchen garbage can is an unsightly item, so it's usually hidden under the sink where it's hard to use.

You can make a built-in garbage container that is easy to use and keeps the garbage hidden (Illus. 193). One container is similar to a pullout shelf. The existing door is removed from the cabinet and reused on the front of the pullout. A frame under the shelf supports the top and provides mounting for the hardware and for the door. A plastic garbage

Illus. 194. A small spring-loaded door can be used as a garbage drop when used with a garbage pail hidden behind the cabinet door.

container fits into a hole cut in the shelf. There is a handhold on each side of the cutout so you can lift the container out to empty it. See project 40.

Another accessory makes use of a spring-loaded dummy drawer front (Illus. 194). The garbage container is placed in the cabinet below, but you don't need to open the door to drop in the garbage. Spring-loaded hinges attach the dummy drawer front to the inside top of the cabinet. Push in on the drawer front and drop the garbage into the container below. See project 41.

Can Rotators

If you keep many canned goods on hand, it's a good practice to use the oldest cans first. The system shown (Illus. 195)

Illus. 195. A can rotator is an easy way to keep canned goods organized. New cans are placed in the top. When you use a can, remove it from the bottom. This automatically rotates the cans so that the oldest ones are used first.

does this automatically. New cans are dropped in the top, and you take the oldest cans out from the bottom. The units use a solid shelf set at an angle to roll the cans down to the lower level. You can build the unit to accept any size can. Usually you will want several sizes to fit the types of cans you intend to store. See project 42.

Illus. 196. Plastic drawer dividers are available, but you can make a custom divider from wood that looks "classy" and can be designed to fit your needs.

Drawer Organizers

When everything is left loose to roll around in a drawer, it can be hard to find what you want when you want it. Drawer organizers keep everything in place. You can buy commercial units made of wire or plastic, or you can build custom dividers from wood (Illus. 196). The advantage of making your own dividers is that you can custom-design the dividers to fit your needs. See project 43. A shallow silverware tray can be added to a drawer and still leave room below for storage. The tray slides on cleats added to the drawer sides. To get to the drawer below, either slide the tray back or lift it out.

By building a special set of dividers, you can use a drawer to keep your spices organized. See project 44.

Vertical Cabinet Partitions

Trays, cookie sheets and shallow pans usually end up piled one on top of another inside a cabinet. Invariably, the first one you will need to use is at the bottom of the pile. Create an organized storage space for these large flat items by adding

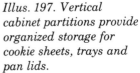

Illus. 197. Vertical cabinet partitions provide organized storage for cookie sheets, trays and pan lids.

Illus. 198. Vertical cabinet partitions can be placed in a narrow cabinet that would otherwise be of limited storage value.

vertical partitions to a cabinet (Illus. 197). The pans and trays slide into the slots and lean against the partitions. You can easily remove or replace any item without disturbing the others. Vertical partitions are a good way to make use of a

Illus. 199. Project 34 plans.

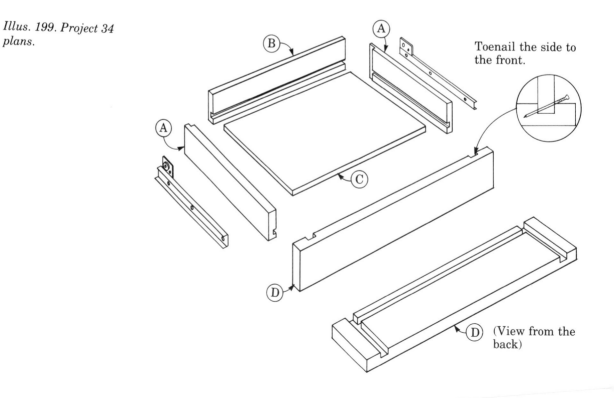

narrow cabinet that would otherwise be of little storage value (Illus. 198).

When building new cabinets, it is easy to add a few dadoes in the shelves for vertical partitions; but different methods are needed when working with existing cabinets. You can add vertical partitions in several ways. See project 45. One way is to make a wood track that attaches to the top and bottom of the cabinet. The divider slides into the track. Another method uses adjustable clips that fit into holes drilled in the top and bottom of the cabinet.

Projects

PROJECT 34—PULLOUT SHELF

This pullout shelf is made from standard materials and uses drawer guides, so you shouldn't have any trouble finding the parts (Illus. 199). The shelf is made from ½" plywood or particleboard. The frame around the shelf is made from 1 × 4 lumber.

Measure the size of the opening to determine the shelf size; then subtract the clearance needed for the guides, (usually ½" per side) so subtract 1". You must account for the sides of the frame. The shelf rests in a ⅜" deep groove; this leaves ⅜" that must be subtracted from each side. The total amount to subtract from the width of the opening is 1¾". The front-to-back measurement doesn't need to allow for the guides, so you only need to subtract ¾" from the inside dimension of the cabinet. Cut the shelf from ½" plywood or particleboard.

The frame is made from 1 × 4 lumber. Cut the parts to length, then cut the joints. The shelf fits into a groove in the frame. Set the dado blade on a table saw to make a ½" wide by ⅜" deep cut ¾" in from the bottom edge of the boards. All four sides are grooved, but the groove in the front is blind. To make the blind groove, notice where the blade begins to project above the table at both the front and the back; make a mark on the fence with a pencil at both of these points. Place marks on the front face of the board where the groove should start and stop. Begin the cut by lowering the board onto the saw at the point where the first mark on the board aligns with the rear mark on the fence. Make sure to keep your fingers well away from the saw blade during this operation. When the board is flat on the table, push it through normally until the second mark on the board aligns with the front mark on the fence. Turn off the saw at this point and wait for the blade to stop, then remove the board. Keep the board pressed down firmly with a push stick as the blade stops. If you don't want to bother with the blind groove, just make the groove all the way along the board. You can let the exposed groove show, or you can cut filler strips and glue them into the ends of the groove.

A rabbet is used to join the sides (Part A) to the back (Part B). Set the dado blade to make a ¾″ wide by ⅜″ deep rabbet and cut the joint. The front (Part D) overhangs the sides by ½″; this conceals the drawer guides. The sides fit into dadoes in the front. The dadoes are ¾″ wide and ⅜″ deep. After cutting the dadoes in the front, you can assemble the shelf. All of the joints are glued, including the groove that the shelf fits into. Drive finish nails into the rabbets at the rear to secure those joints. The dadoes in the front are locked with finish nails toenailed in from the side. Hold the nail at an angle and drive it in from the side so that it will go through the side and into the front on the other side of the dado. Use a nailset to drive the nail at the end when you can't get the hammer in close enough.

Follow the manufacturer's directions for installing the drawer guides, then slide the shelf into the cabinet.

Project 34
Pullout Shelf

BILL OF MATERIALS

Note: Dimension A is the width of the cabinet opening. Dimension B is the depth of the opening. The first bill of materials can be used to figure dimensions for any size opening. The others are for specific sizes.

Part	Description	Size	No. Req'd
A	sides	¾ × 3⅝ × B- ⅜	2
B	back	¾ × 3⅝ × A-1 ¾	1
C	shelf	½ × A- 1¾ × B- ¾	1
D	front	¾ × 3⅝ × A- ¼	1

Fits opening 13½″ wide and 23″ deep

Part	Description	Size	No. Req'd
A	sides	¾ × 3⅝ × 22⅝	2
B	back	¾ × 3⅝ × 11¾	1
C	shelf	½ × 11¾ × 22¼	1
D	front	¾ × 3⅝ × 13¼	1

Fits opening 16½″ wide and 23″ deep

Part	Description	Size	No. Req'd
A	sides	¾ × 3⅝ × 22⅝	2
B	back	¾ × 3⅝ × 14¾	1
C	shelf	½ × 14¾ × 22¼	1
D	front	¾ × 3⅝ × 16¼	1

Fits opening 22½″ wide and 23″ deep

Part	Description	Size	No. Req'd
A	sides	¾ × 3⅝ × 22⅝	2
B	back	¾ × 3⅝ × 20¾	1
C	shelf	½ × 20¾ × 22¼	1
D	front	¾ × 3⅝ × 22¼	1

Fits opening 28½″ wide and 23″ deep

Part	Description	Size	No. Req'd
A	sides	¾ × 3⅝ × 22⅝	2
B	back	¾ × 3⅝ × 26¾	1
C	shelf	½ × 26¾ × 22¼	1
D	front	¾ × 3⅝ × 28¼	1

Fits opening 34½″ wide and 23″ deep

Part	Description	Size	No. Req'd
A	sides	¾ × 3⅝ × 22⅝	2
B	back	¾ × 3⅝ × 32¾	1
C	shelf	½ × 32¾ × 22¼	1
D	front	¾ × 3⅝ × 34¼	1

PROJECT 35—LAZY SUSANS

A lazy Susan makes a corner cabinet more efficient, because you can easily get to all of the storage space simply by rotating the shelf. There are several types of hardware kits available, and they can be used with different types of doors. When the cabinet front is angled across the corner, you can use full circle shelves. This is usually the most convenient, because you can shut the door with the shelf in any position. When the cabinet has a square corner, the shelves must have a notched-out section. The doors can only be closed when this section is aligned with the opening. There are three types of doors that can be used with a square corner. The first type (Illus. 200), the most convenient to use, has doors that are attached to the shelves and rotate with the lazy Susan. Push-

Illus. 200. When the doors are attached directly to the lazy Susan, the unit is very convenient to use, but there is a visible gap around the doors when the unit is closed.

Illus. 201. Lipped or overlay doors can be used on a lazy Susan opening. The method shown uses two doors hinged on opposite sides.

Illus. 202. Another way to attach the doors is to use a piano hinge in the center to connect the two doors, then attach one of the doors to the cabinet using standard cabinet hinges.

ing in on one door rotates the shelves. Even though this is the most convenient to use, it isn't always visually pleasing. There will be a small, but visible gap between the doors and face frame. When the rest of the doors are the lipped or overlay types, you may want to use the same type on the lazy Susan opening. The doors can be hinged on both sides of the opening as shown (Illus. 201), or you can hinge them together in the center using a piano hinge, and then attach one side to the cabinet with a standard cabinet hinge as shown (Illus. 202).

Once you have removed any fixed shelves, installing the lazy Susan hardware is fairly simple. Screw pivots to the top and to the bottom of the cabinet (Illus. 203). The center pole may need to be cut to length, or it may be adjustable (Illus. 204). Slide the shelves onto the pole and insert the pole into the pivots. The exact procedure will vary, so follow the manufacturer's directions. After the pole is secured, the shelves

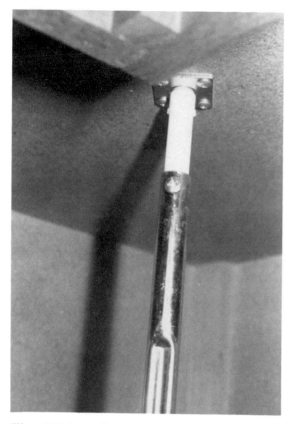

Illus. 203. Lazy Susan installation is fairly simple. The shelves are attached to the center pole, then the pivots are attached with screws to the top and bottom of the cabinet.

Illus. 204. This center pole is adjustable. It fits a variety of cabinet heights without modification.

can be adjusted to any position by first loosening the set screw, moving the shelf, and then retightening the set screw (Illus. 205).

PROJECT 36—LAZY SUSAN FOR AN EXISTING SHELF

If your cabinets have fixed shelves, you may not want to tear them out to add a lazy Susan. You can add a lazy Susan to the top of an existing shelf by using a special type of bearing plate (Illus. 206). The bearing plate consists of two metal

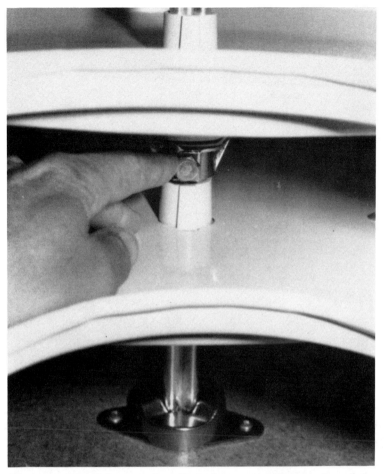

Illus. 205. The shelves can be adjusted to any position on the pole by loosening the set screw and retightening it once the shelf is in position.

plates that are pivoted in the center and ride on ball bearings. Cut the new lazy Susan shelf out of plywood. Measure the inside of the cabinet and decide on the largest circle that will fit. Mark the circle on the plywood and use a sabre saw to cut it out.

Attach the bearing plate to the underside of the new shelf using screws. Make sure that the plate is centered. Turn the free part of the plate so that the corners are out of alignment with the other half. This puts the screw holes where you can get to them. Push an awl through one of the holes to mark the location of the screw hole on the underside of the new shelf. Drill a ¾″ diameter hole in this location. This will give you an access hole to attach the bottom plate to the existing shelf.

Illus. 206. You can use a lazy Susan bearing plate to add a lazy Susan on top of an existing shelf. Attach the bearing to the underside of the circular shelf using screws, then position the lazy Susan on the existing shelf. A hole in the lazy Susan allows access to the screw holes in the lower part of the bearing plate so that the unit can be attached to the shelf.

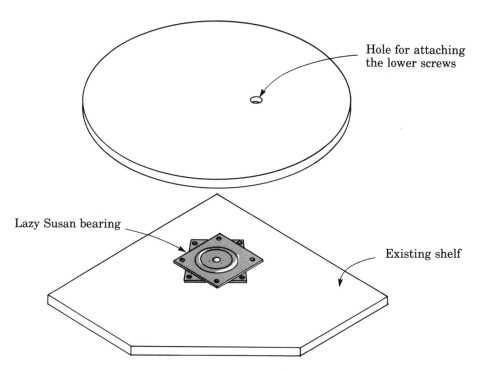

Hole for attaching the lower screws

Lazy Susan bearing

Existing shelf

A metal rim around the shelf prevents things from falling off as you rotate the shelf. Buy a 1″ wide strip of aluminum that has predrilled holes. Bend the aluminum around the outside of the shelf and cut it off where the ends meet. Attach the strip to the shelf using small screws.

Place the lazy Susan in the cabinet and position it so that it turns freely. Shine a flashlight through the hole in the shelf and look for the screw holes as you slowly rotate the shelf. When the hole aligns with one of the screw holes, put a screw on the end of a magnetic screwdriver. A Phillips head screw will be easier to use than a standard slotted type. Use the screwdriver through the hole in the shelf to place the screw in the bearing plate hole, then drive the screw into the existing shelf. Rotate the shelf to the next hole and repeat the procedure. When all four screws are in place, the shelf is ready to use.

PROJECT 37—STORAGE BIN FRONT

Storage bins can have solid fronts, but a glass or wire grill insert can make the front of the bin decorative and it will allow you to see the contents. The wire grill front also allows for ventilation.

The frame for the front is made from ¾″ thick solid lumber (Illus. 207). Begin by ripping the stock to 2″ in width, then cut the parts to length. The length of the stiles (Part A) is equal to the overall height of the front. The length of the rails (Part B) is equal to the overall width of the front minus 4″.

Assemble the frame using blind dowel joints at the corners. Apply glue to the joints and dowel holes, then assemble and

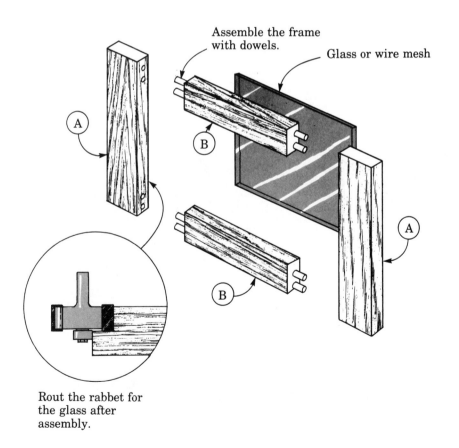

Assemble the frame with dowels.

Glass or wire mesh

A

B

A

B

Rout the rabbet for the glass after assembly.

Illus. 207. Project 37 plans.

clamp using bar clamps. After removing it from the clamps, rout out a rabbet inside the opening. Use a rabbeting bit that has a pilot bearing. The pilot will ride along the inside edge of the frame and guide the cut. The router will round the corners. Use a chisel to square them up.

The fronts can be used with both types of bins (project 38 or 39). The next step is to cut the dadoes in the stiles that will join the sides to the front. When used with project 38, you will also need to cut a groove for the bottom.

Finish the frame to match the cabinets. Install the glass or wire grill after the front is attached to the bin. Hold it in the opening with a wood or plastic stop.

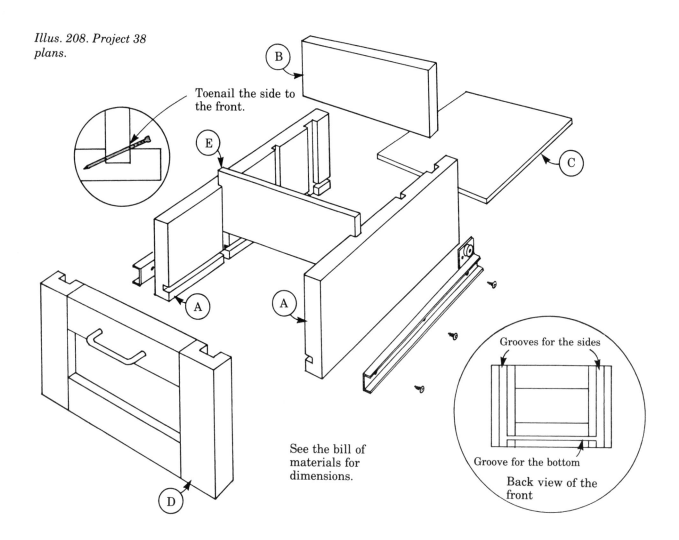

Illus. 208. Project 38 plans.

Toenail the side to the front.

See the bill of materials for dimensions.

Grooves for the sides

Groove for the bottom

Back view of the front

PROJECT 38—STORAGE BIN WITH DIVIDERS

This storage bin is built much like a drawer. Adjustable dividers make it possible to store several items in one bin. Make the fronts following the directions in project 37.

The sides and back can be made from ½″ thick solid lumber or plywood (Illus. 208). Begin by ripping the sides (Part A) to width, and then cut them to length; then set the dado blade on a table saw to cut a ½″ wide by ¼″ deep dado. Cut the dado in the ends of the sides ¾″ in from the end.

Reset the dado blade to make a ¼″ wide by ¼″ deep cut. Cut the groove for the bottom in both sides and the front, then cut the dadoes for the adjustable dividers. You can position the dividers however you like; but make sure that the dadoes are in the same position on both sides. To do this, add an extension fence to the mitre gauge on the saw. Make the extension fence from a piece of plywood about 2″ wide and a little longer than the side of the bin. Attach the fence to the mitre gauge by driving through the holes in the gauge. Clamp a block of wood to the fence to position the cut. Butt the end of the side against the block and make the dado. When you cut the dado in the other side, make sure that the same end is against the block. Reposition the block and make the next set of dadoes.

The back (Part B) isn't as wide as the sides. The bottom edge should be flush with the top of the groove in the sides. Assemble the bin using glue and finish nails. Drive the nails through the sides and into the back. The front is attached by toenailing through the side into the front. It's a good idea to drill a pilot hole for the nail by using a bit that is slightly smaller than the nail.

The bottom of the bin (Part C) is made from ¼″ thick plywood or particleboard. Slide the bottom into the groove from the back. Square up the bin, then drive small box nails through the bottom into the back of the bin. The dividers are cut from ¼″ thick plywood or hardboard. Slide them into the dadoes in the sides. The interior of the bin should be finished using a nontoxic (salad bowl) finish.

Attach the drawer guides to the bin and slide the bin into the cabinet.

Project 38
Storage Bin with Dividers

BILL OF MATERIALS

Note: Dimensions allow for ½″ clearance on sides for drawer guide.

Fits opening 10½″ wide × 6½″ high × 23″ deep

Part	Description	Size	No. Req'd
A	sides	½ × 6 × 22	2
B	back	½ × 5¼ × 9	1
C	bottom	¼ × 9 × 21¼	1
D	front	¾ × 7½ × 11½	1
E	dividers	¼ × 5 × 9	varies

Fits opening 13½″ wide × 6½″ high × 23″ deep

Part	Description	Size	No. Req'd
A	sides	½ × 6 × 22	2
B	back	½ × 5¼ × 11	1
C	bottom	¼ × 11 × 21¼	1
D	front	¾ × 7½ × 14½	1
E	dividers	¼ × 5 × 11	varies

PROJECT 39—TILT-OUT BINS

Tilt-out bins are useful when the bins are positioned behind a counter. You can tilt open the bin without removing everything from the counter in front (Illus. 209).

Illus. 209. A tilt-out bin can be used behind a counter. Because it tilts out, you don't need to remove everything from the counter in order to open the bin.

Build the fronts as described in project 37. The sides (Part A) are cut from ¼″ plywood (Illus. 210). To lay out the sides, mark the height of the front minus 1″ along one edge of the piece of plywood. Use a pair of dividers to mark the curved cut along the top. Set the dividers to the height of the side. Place one point on the mark and scratch a curve with the other point. From the same point that you need to mark the curve, draw a 60° line to intersect the curve. You now have the outline of the side. Cut it out with a sabre saw. Trace around the first side to lay out the rest.

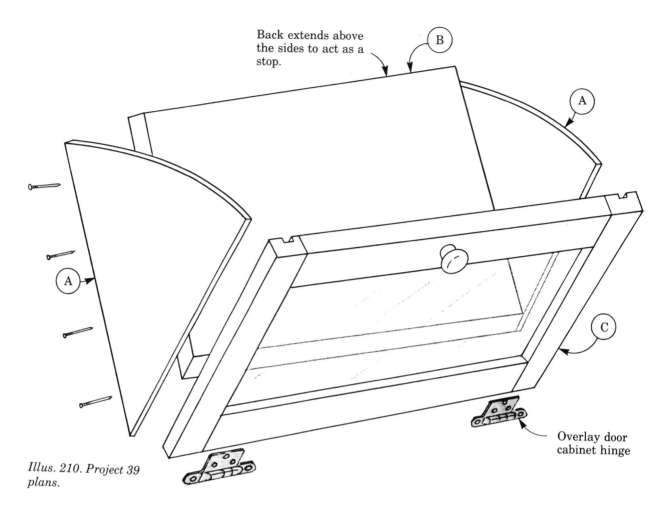

Back extends above
the sides to act as a
stop.

*Illus. 210. Project 39
plans.*

Overlay door
cabinet hinge

Apply glue to the dadoes in the bin front and install the sides. Drill pilot holes and toenail through the sides into the front. The back is made from ½" thick plywood. Notice that it is ¾" taller than the sides. The back acts as a stop; when the back hits the inside of the face frame, it prevents the bin from opening too far. Before installing the back, attach the hinges to the back of the bin front. Use full overlay type cabinet hinges. Now place the back on the sides. Attach the back using glue and nails. Finish the interior of the bin with a nontoxic finish.

Slide the bin into the face frame and attach the hinges to the face frame.

Project 39
Tilt-out Bins

BILL OF MATERIALS
Fits opening 15″ wide × 12″ high × 12″ deep

Part	Description	Size	No. Req'd
A	sides	¼ × 10½ × 11½	2
B	back	½ × 12½ × 14¼	1
C	front	¾ × 16 × 12½	1

Fits opening 18″ wide × 12″ high × 12″ deep

Part	Description	Size	No. Req'd
A	sides	¼ × 10½ × 11½	2
B	back	½ × 12½ × 17¼	1
C	front	¾ × 19 × 12½	1

PROJECT 40—PULLOUT GARBAGE BIN

This pullout garbage bin conceals the garbage container and also makes it convenient to use (Illus. 211). First choose one of the base cabinets for the installation. Measure the space available and buy a plastic garbage container that will fit into the cabinet.

Remove the door from the cabinet and remove the hinges. The door will be reattached later to conceal the garbage bin. The top (Part A) is made from ¾″ thick plywood. Trace around the plastic garbage container to get the outline of the opening. Make the opening smaller than the lip on the container so that the top will support the container by the lip. Draw in two hand holes on the sides so that the container can be easily removed. Use a sabre saw to cut out the opening.

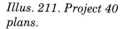

Illus. 211. Project 40 plans.

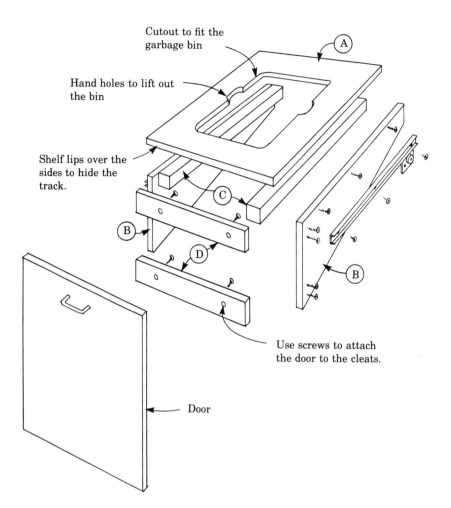

Next cut the sides (Part B) from ½″ thick plywood. The bottom of the side is angled to save materials and to make the unit lighter. Cut the two pieces of 2 × 2 (Part C) and attach them to the underside of the top using glue and screws. The 2 × 2s are set in from the edges to allow for the sides and the clearance for the drawer guides. The drawer guide usually needs ½″ clearance, so set Part C back 1″ from the edge. The front end of Part C should be set back ¾″ from the front edge of the top.

Attach the sides (Part B) to the 2 × 2s (Part C) using glue and nails. The front edge of the side should be flush with the front edge of the top. Attach the door mounting cleats (Part D) to the sides at the top and the bottom. Install the drawer guides following the manufacturer's directions, and slide the unit into the cabinet.

Once the unit is in the cabinet, you can then position the door. You can mark the location of the screw holes using dowel centers. Drill ¼″ diameter holes in the mounting cleats (Part D) and insert dowel centers. Place the door in position; when you are satisfied with the alignment, press in hard on the door; the points of the dowel centers will leave a mark on the door. Drill a pilot hole at each mark, then pull out the unit and drive screws through the mounting cleats into the back of the door.

Drop the plastic container into the outlined hole in the top, and the pullout garbage bin is ready for use.

Project 40
Pullout Garbage Bin

BILL OF MATERIALS
Fits opening 13½″ wide × 23″ deep

Part	Description	Size	No. Req'd
A	top	¾ × 13¼ × 22	1
B	sides	½ × 15 × 22	2
C	braces	1⅝ × 1⅝ × 21¼	2
D	cleats	¾ × 3 × 11½	2

Fits opening 16½″ wide × 23″ deep

Part	Description	Size	No. Req'd
A	top	¾ × 16¼ × 22	1
B	sides	½ × 15 × 22	2
C	braces	1⅝ × 1⅝ × 21¼	2
D	cleats	¾ × 3 × 14½	2

PROJECT 41—SPRING-LOADED GARBAGE DROP

This garbage drop makes use of a dummy drawer front. The garbage container sits in the cabinet below. The drawer front is hinged so that you can push in on the front and drop the garbage into the container.

If there is a dummy drawer front in your cabinets that has enough clearance behind it to allow the door to swing in, you can use it as a garbage drop. The dummy drawer fronts by the sink usually won't work, because the sink will interfere with the operation of the door. If there isn't a suitable dummy drawer front, you may have to sacrifice a drawer. If the cabinets have a face frame around the dummy drawer opening, the face frame will need to be modified. This project works best in cabinets constructed without face frames.

First remove the drawer front; it will be used as the door to the garbage drop. If there is a face frame, use a fine saw to cut out the bottom rail in the opening. Attach the piece of face

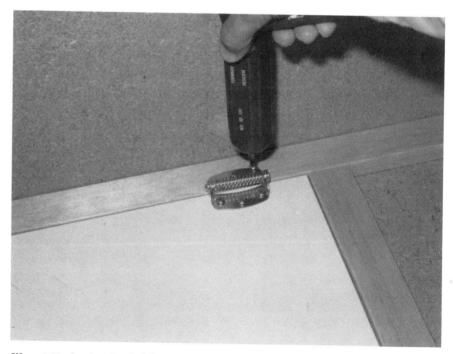

Illus. 212. Spring-loaded hinges are used to attach the top edge of the garbage-drop door to the inside of the cabinet face frame.

frame that you removed to the back of the door. Position it as it would have been positioned originally, and then secure it using glue and nails.

Any other parts of the face frame or mounting cleats that would prevent the door from opening inward should be cut away.

The hinges are spring-loaded. Attach the hinges to the back of the door, position the door in the cabinet, and then attach the hinges to the cabinet (Illus. 212). If the door springs out past the front of the cabinet, attach a steel strip to the back of the door that will hit the face frame and stop the door from swinging out too far. Place the garbage container directly below the door and the garbage drop is ready to use.

If there isn't a suitable drawer front in the location you want to use, you can modify an existing cabinet door to make a garbage drop. Remove the door from the cabinet and saw off an 8″ section from the top. Smooth any rough edges using sandpaper, and then finish the edges to match the rest of the cabinet. Reposition the top hinge on the door so that it is attached to the lower section. Attach the top portion of the door to the cabinet using spring-loaded hinges along the top edge. Reattach the lower section of the door to the cabinet, and then place the garbage container inside the cabinet.

PROJECT 42—CAN ROTATOR

When you store many of the same types of canned goods, a can rotator conserves' shelf space and ensures that you always use the oldest cans first (Illus. 213). You can modify the plans to accept any size can; make dimension "A" slightly larger than the can diameter, and make the width of the opening slightly wider than the height of the can (Illus. 214).

The sides of the unit (Part A) and back (Part C) are made from ⅛″ hardboard; I used some scraps of hardboard wood

Illus. 213. Sloping shelves inside the can rotator guide the cans from the upper opening to the lower opening.

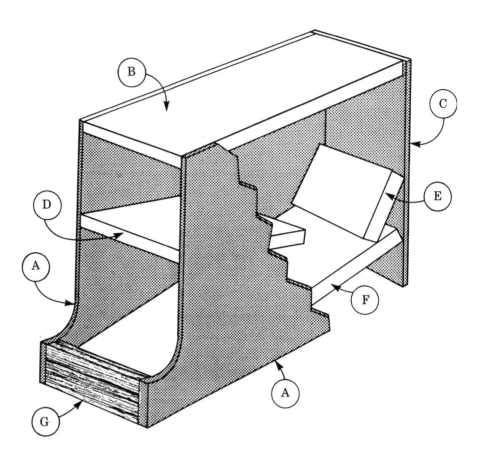

panelling to make the project look a bit nicer, but standard hardboard will work. The rest of the parts are cut from ½″ plywood or particleboard.

Parts B,C,D,E,F and G are all of the same width. Set the table saw and rip some pieces, then cut the parts to length.

You will probably want to make several can rotators at once, so it pays to make a simple jig to speed up the assembly (Illus. 215). Lay out the location of all of the parts on a scrap of particleboard, then nail strips of wood to the particleboard to hold the parts in position. Put the parts into the slots on the jig and apply glue to the exposed edges. Place one of the sides (Part A) on top of the parts in the jig and drive a few panelling nails through the side into the interior guides

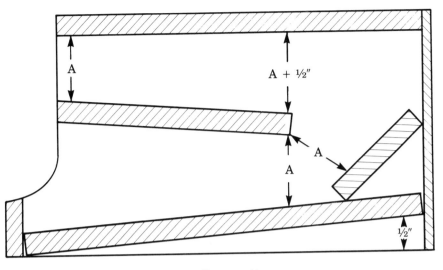

A + ½"

A

A

½"

Cross section

Illus. 214. Project 42 plans. Dimension A is slightly larger than the diameter of the can.

(Parts D, E and F) and into the top (Part B). Remove the unit from the jig and install the other side and the back (Part C).

You can leave the unit unfinished, or you can paint it or apply stain and varnish. If you want to dress it up, you can apply wood veneer tape to the exposed edges.

To use the can rotator, drop cans into the opening at the top; they will roll down the shelf and appear at the lower

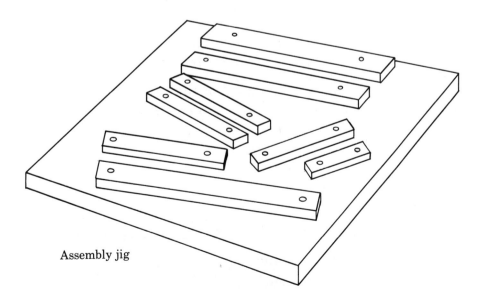

Assembly jig

Illus. 215. An assembly jig can speed up the process when you are making several can rotators. Tack strips of wood to a plywood base. The strips hold the can guides in proper position while one of the sides is attached, then the unit can be removed from the jig and the other side attached.

opening. When you want to use a can, remove it from the lower opening. A new can will roll down to replace it. As you buy new cans, add them to the upper opening. This will keep your can supply always fresh, and you will use the oldest cans first.

Project 42
Can Rotator

BILL OF MATERIALS
For cans 2¾″ diameter × 4″ high

Part	Description	Size	No. Req'd
A	sides	⅛ × 8 × 11	2
B	top	½ × 4¼ × 10	1
C	back	⅛ × 4½ × 8	1
D	center guide	½ × 4¼ × 6	1
E	rear guide	½ × 4¼ × 2¾	1
F	bottom	½ × 4¼ × 10¼	1
G	front stop	½ × 4¼ × 1	1

For cans 3⅛″ diameter × 4⅜″ high

Part	Description	Size	No. Req'd
A	sides	⅛ × 9 × 11	2
B	top	½ × 4⅝ × 10	1
C	back	⅛ × 4⅞ × 9	1
D	center guide	½ × 4⅝ × 5¾	1
E	rear guide	½ × 4⅝ × 2¾	1
F	bottom	½ × 4⅝ × 10¼	1
G	front stop	½ × 4⅝ × 1	1

PROJECT 43—DRAWER DIVIDERS

Drawer dividers provide individual storage spaces for items such as silverware and cutlery. You could buy a plastic divider, but by making you own from wood, you can customize the divider to suit your needs, and the wood divider looks elegant.

The divider is made from ½″ thick solid lumber (Illus. 216). All of the parts are of the same width, so begin by ripping some pieces to the correct width. Make the divider about ¼″ smaller than the inside drawer dimension, and allow ¼″ for the plywood bottom. Next, cut the parts to length. Cut rabbets ½″ wide by ¼″ inch deep in the ends of the sides (Part A). Also cut a ½″ wide by ¼″ deep dado in each side for Part C. Parts B and C are dadoed to accept the dividers. Make ½″ wide by ¼″ deep dadoes at the desired locations.

Begin assembly by applying glue to the dadoes in Parts B and C and inserting the dividers. Apply glue to the joints in

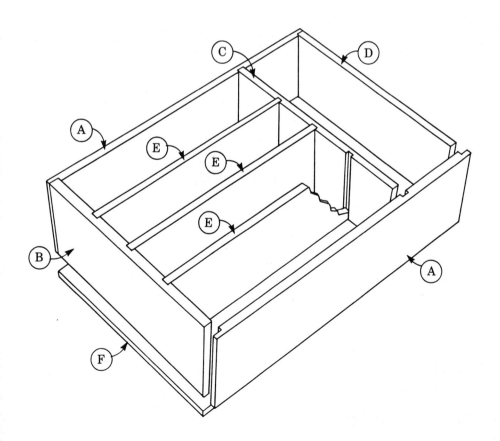

Illus. 216. Project 43 plans.

the sides (Part A), and insert parts B, C and D into the joints on A. Drive a few finish nails through the side into B, C and D. Square up the assembly, then attach the ¼″ plywood bottom using glue and some brads.

You can improve and organize a deep drawer by adding a sliding tray. The tray sits on cleats attached to the sides of the drawer. You can store small items in the tray where they are easy to find and still have room under the tray for larger items. The length of the tray is half the length of the drawer, so you can slide it back to get to the items underneath. You can also lift the tray out when you need more access to the lower part of the drawer.

Build the tray following the directions above. You may want to cut a finger pull in the front (Part B) to make it easy to grab the tray to slide it back and forth.

Use a piece of ½″ thick solid lumber to make the cleats that attach to the side of the drawer. Attach the cleats with short screws to the inside of the drawer. Place the tray on the cleats. You should be able to slide the tray freely along the cleats. Rub some paraffin wax on the top edge of the cleat to make the tray slide smoothly.

PROJECT 44—SPICE DRAWER

If your spices are in attractive bottles, a spice rack can be a decorative addition to a kitchen. If you use spices that come in rectangular metal tins, you want them handy but not necessarily on display. This spice drawer will keep your spices organized and easy to reach, but when you close the drawer, the tins are hidden (Illus. 217).

This is a very simple project that requires only a slight modification of an existing drawer. Cut lengths of cove moulding to fit between the sides of the drawer. Put one of the strips in the drawer and place a spice tin on the front row. Adjust the position of the moulding so that the tin rests against it at an angle. The top of the tins slightly overlap the bottom of the tins in the next higher row to conserve space.

Illus. 217. With the addition of a simple rack, a drawer can be used for organized spice storage.

The moulding is positioned so that the flat edge is pointed towards the back of the drawer so that the bottom of the tins on the next higher row rest against the flat edge. Adjust the position of the moulding up and down and back and forth until you get the proper tilt and overlap, then mark the location. Remove the tins and drive a finish nail through the side of the drawer into the ends of the moulding (Illus. 218).

Illus. 218. The spice tins lean against pieces of cove moulding nailed inside the drawer. Determine the location of the moulding by experimenting with the position of the spice tins. Attach the moulding by driving a small finish nail through the side of the drawer into the end of the moulding.

You can add just a few strips to the front of the drawer, or you can fill the drawer with rows of spice tins. When you load the drawer, all of the cans are easy to lift out and all of the labels are visible.

PROJECT 45—VERTICAL CABINET PARTITIONS

A vertical partition in a cabinet can be used as a storage rack for trays, cookie sheets and other large flat pans or pot lids (Illus. 219). An easy way to add partitions to an existing cabinet is to use a wood track (Illus. 220). The track is made from ¾″ thick solid lumber. Rip a strip 1″ wide, and then cut a groove in the center that will fit the partition.

Illus. 219. Add vertical partitions to an existing cabinet to organize the storage of large flat pans and cookie sheets.

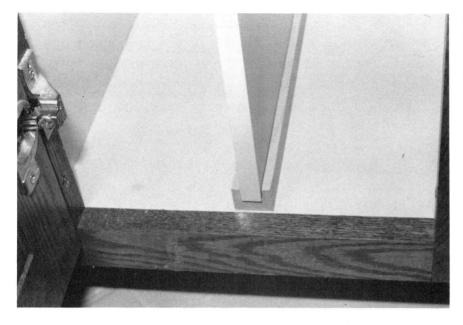

Illus. 220. A wood track attached to the top and bottom of the cabinet can be used to support the vertical partition.

Place the track inside the cabinet in the desired position. Drill and countersink screw holes through the bottom of the groove in the track. Use flathead screws to attach one track to the top and another to the bottom of the cabinet.

Cut the partition to fit inside the track, and slide it in place (Illus. 221). The partition is left loose so you can slide it out if you decide to change the arrangement of the cabinet or if you need to get to the back of the cabinet for cleaning.

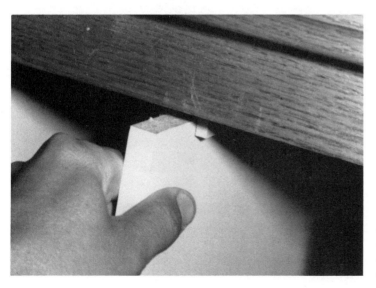

Illus. 221. The partition can be left loose in the track. This allows you to remove the partitions to clean, or to rearrange your storage areas.

An easy way to add adjustable partitions is to use a special type of clip (Illus. 222). This clip is designed to support adjustable shelves, but because it has a locking feature, it also works well for vertical partitions. Drill a series of holes in the top and the bottom of the cabinet. The holes must line up with each other front to back and top to bottom. An easy way to lay out the holes is to use a piece of pegboard as a drill guide. Cut a strip of pegboard that will fit inside the cabinet. Position the guide along the line where you want the holes drilled in the cabinet. In this example, I'll start on the bottom along the front edge. Butt one end of the guide against the side of the cabinet. Now drill through each hole with a ¼″ drill bit. You don't need to use every hole. You can skip some holes to increase the spacing. If you skip holes, make a mark by the ones you will use. Reposition the guide at the rear of the cabinet, keeping the end against the same side of the cabinet. Drill the next series of holes. Now repeat the procedure for the top of the cabinet. Make sure that the end is against the same side of the cabinet as it was on the bottom. When drilling the top hole, it is important to use a stop on the drill. If you drill the holes too deep, you run the risk of drilling through the countertop.

Illus. 222. This clip is designed as a shelf support. Because of the locking feature, it can also be used with vertical partitions.

Metric Equivalents

INCHES TO MILLIMETRES AND CENTIMETRES

MM—millimetres   CM—centimetres

Inches	MM	CM	Inches	CM	Inches	CM
⅛	3	0.3	9	22.9	30	76.2
¼	6	0.6	10	25.4	31	78.7
⅜	10	1.0	11	27.9	32	81.3
½	13	1.3	12	30.5	33	83.8
⅝	16	1.6	13	33.0	34	86.4
¾	19	1.9	14	35.6	35	88.9
⅞	22	2.2	15	38.1	36	91.4
1	25	2.5	16	40.6	37	94.0
1¼	32	3.2	17	43.2	38	96.5
1½	38	3.8	18	45.7	39	99.1
1¾	44	4.4	19	48.3	40	101.6
2	51	5.1	20	50.8	41	104.1
2½	64	6.4	21	53.3	42	106.7
2	76	7.6	22	55.9	43	109.2
3½	89	8.9	23	58.4	44	111.8
4	102	10.2	24	61.0	45	114.3
4½	114	11.4	25	63.5	46	116.8
5	127	12.7	26	66.0	47	119.4
6	152	15.2	27	68.6	48	121.9
7	178	17.8	28	71.1	49	124.5
8	203	20.3	29	73.7	50	127.0

About the Author

Sam Allen began building custom cabinets for friends and relatives while he was still in high school. In his senior year, he was chosen to represent his school in a statewide industrial arts competition. He earned money for college by building cabinets for a local unfinished-furniture store.

After graduating from Brigham Young University with a Bachelor of Science degree in Industrial Education, he worked as a carpenter and cabinetmaker, gaining experience in both custom and mass-production cabinetmaking techniques.

His appreciation of hand-tool techniques and antique reproductions began with his study of the cabinets and furniture produced by the early settlers of his native state, Utah. The dry climate of Utah tends to exaggerate problems caused by wood movement; this has led Mr. Allen to extensively study and experiment with techniques that will minimize these problems.

Mr. Allen is a widely published free-lance writer. He is the author of the book, *Wood Finisher's Handbook*, and he has had numerous articles in magazines, such as *Popular Mechanics, The Woodworker's Journal, Fine Woodworking*, and *Popular Woodworker*.

INDEX